Dearest Arlette:

Everyday Life in Postwar America and France,
1945-1955,
as Recorded in the Letters of Two Reunited Families

To Cathy and Bill with love always and many happy Bay High memories!

Emily de Montluzin

and

Emmie de Montluzin

11/14/11

1. Emily de Montluzin and Arlette Delattre before Arlette's reception at Hotel Reed in Bay St. Louis, MS (Summer 1948)

Dearest Arlette:

Everyday Life in Postwar America and France,
1945-1955,
as Recorded in the Letters of Two Reunited Families

Emily Hosmer de Montluzin
with
Emily Lorraine de Montluzin

The R. L. Bryan Company
301 Greystone Blvd.
Columbia, SC 29210

Copyright © 2011 by Emily Hosmer de Montluzin
and Emily Lorraine de Montluzin
All rights reserved.
ISBN: 978-1-4507-9057-4

To
Georges and Jeannine Delattre

Contents

To the Reader	ix
Acknowledgments	xiii
I. In the Beginning	1
II. Two Home Fronts: 1945-1948	7
III. Interlude: Summer 1948	64
IV. New Times, New Challenges: 1948-1955	70
V. The End of the Story	166

To the Reader

This volume consists of the letters written by Emily Hosmer de Montluzin, then of Bay St. Louis, Mississippi, to her young French cousin by marriage, Arlette Delattre, during the first decade after World War II, with a handful of Arlette's surviving letters commingled. The correspondence of Emily and Arlette showcases the experience of two ordinary families, one American and one French, as their countries were adjusting to the political and international challenges, economic stresses, and social changes of a postwar world. These letters constitute, in short, a window into the daily life and attitudes of the two correspondents—into world news events discussed, political opinions aired, economic conditions confronted, books read, films enjoyed, the daily comings and goings of family and social life. As such, they reflect the marked differences between the American experience in the aftermath of war and that of France, especially during the late 1940s.

While broad generalizations should not be overdrawn, postwar America, though beset initially by strikes, rationing, and shortages, was a triumphant country imbued with vibrant optimism. The national mood was reflected not only in the Baby Boom and in a burgeoning consumer society but also in a universal sense of relief from the grinding anxiety of war and a determination on the part of demobilized servicemen and their families to revel in entertainment. The result was a headlong rush to socialize—to establish or join clubs, give coffee parties, host bridge games, see movies, go to dances, or take part in community theatre—a tamer, saner version, in a word, of the frivolity of the Roaring 'Twenties, itself a reaction to the trauma of the First World War. Emily and her husband René were well positioned to participate in the conviviality of the day, since the small town of Bay St. Louis lay midway along the Mississippi Gulf Coast between New Orleans and Biloxi, within easy reach of operas, ballets, plays, and dance orchestras and immersed in the Mardi Gras culture of New Orleans.

France, by contrast, emerged from war as a nation burdened by painful memories of the humiliation of surrender in 1940 and a half-decade of Nazi occupation, a nation with a wrecked economy and widespread hunger only partially ameliorated by packages of food sent by relatives and friends abroad, a nation paralyzed by waves of strikes and political unrest as the Fourth Republic got off to its shaky start. Recovery, to be sure, would come, stimulated by Marshall Plan aid and by bold French and German initiatives that would lead to the European Union and France's economic resurgence in the 'Fifties. The 'Forties, however, were indisputably a dreadful time in the history of France. Nowhere in this correspondence is the difference in national mood more evident than in two letters: one written by Emily on June 12, 1947, in response to Arlette's avid questions, describing excitedly the latest practical inventions for American kitchens (a machine that washed dishes, appliances that washed and dried clothes, ovens with temperature knobs and see-through glass panels in their doors, refrigerators with freezing compartments, etc.) and one written by Arlette on October 2, 1948, after her first visit to the United States, telling Emily that she had returned to a France so filled with political discord, economic strife, and bleakness of outlook that to her grief she was "not any more very proud to be French."

As with all epistolary narratives, the preparation of *Dearest Arlette* necessitated editorial judgments concerning inclusiveness as well as presentation. Virtually all of Emily's letters over the span of a sixty-year correspondence with Arlette are extant, and the decision to limit those included here to the period of 1945-1955 was a difficult one. Subsequent letters deal insightfully with a number of important topics: the Suez Crisis, the Hungarian Revolution of 1956, the Algerian uprising, the 1958 attempted *coup* in Paris, the Kennedy assassination, race relations in the American South, de Gaulle's severing of French participatory ties with NATO, Apollo XI's landing on the Moon, Nixon's trip to China, the Viet Nam War, the Teheran hostage crisis, the War in the Falklands, presidential politics, the fall of the Berlin Wall, the "people power" revolutions in eastern Europe in 1989, the Persian Gulf War, "ethnic cleansing" in Bosnia and Kosovo, the aftermath of the attacks of September 11, and finally the catastrophe of Hurricane Katrina, which decimated the Mississippi Gulf Coast and New Orleans (and destroyed Emily's home) in 2005. The correspondence concluded only with the death of Arlette Delattre Baron in 2006. However, it seemed clear that the letters dating from the first postwar decade offer the greatest concentration of material of both historical value and popular appeal. In addition, the year 1955 afforded a natural personal break point, coinciding as it did with Arlette's marriage. As Emily wrote that summer, Arlette soon would no longer be "Mlle Arlette Delattre," her "little sister," but "Madame Jacques Baron."

In contrast to Emily's letters, only a handful of Arlette's written during the years encompassed in this book survive. Throughout the early decades of her correspondence Arlette, like most of her contemporaries, wrote habitually with a fountain pen. The flood waters of Katrina, while leaving the sodden letters behind, washed her words entirely away. As a result only four from Arlette, one from her father, one from her younger brother Georges, and one from her uncle René dating from this period remain sufficiently legible to decipher, apparently spared from obliteration by the accident of their having been tightly bundled together. Unfortunately those letters do not include the very first that Arlette wrote (and sent in care of the mayor of Bay St. Louis), conveying to her American cousins the news that their family in France had survived the Second World War. Arlette's later letters on the contrary were composed with a ball-point pen or on a typewriter. Retrieved from a flooded cabinet, frozen to kill hurricane-induced mold, and subsequently dried in the sun, they are in nearly perfect condition, but they lie outside the scope of this book.

While the great majority of the 1945-1955 correspondence is preserved in the following pages, not every letter is of sufficient interest to readers to include. Likewise, some passages that are needlessly repetitive or that deal with purely family matters or with inconsequential news of mutual friends have been omitted or condensed, with ellipses scrupulously marked and brief summaries provided where necessary. Except for the correction of occasional inadvertent oversights in spelling and grammar and the modernizing of punctuation, the text of the letters has been preserved as written.

Readers will note that the early letters from Emily to Arlette were consciously written in straightforward declarative style and relatively simple vocabulary in order to facilitate their comprehension by a teenaged girl for whom English was a second language, albeit one in which she was making rapid strides. As Arlette's facility in English grew, the style of Emily's letters became more complex and their vocabulary more wide-ranging. In addition, Emily, as a teacher of French, took care to employ in her letters the formularistic phraseology that in France is a traditional aspect of observing *politesse*: standard conventions of French epistolary style ("your charming letter," "your distinguished father," etc.), common expressions of endearment ("a thousand kisses," "I embrace you," etc.), habitual apologies for "laziness" in not replying sooner to letters, and a carefully observed distinction between Arlette (with whom she could employ the familiar *tu*) and her parents (who are consistently referred to as "Monsieur" and "Madame" and addressed with the formal second-person *vous*).

Footnotes, which are few in number, are designedly factual rather than interpretative, provided simply to offer the necessary historical context for the correspondence that follows and to assist readers in following the circuitous twists and turns of Fourth-Republic France. The intent throughout has been to let the letters tell the story.

E. H. de M. and E. L. de M.

Acknowledgments

The authors would like to express thanks to many friends who have offered encouragement in the course of the completion of this project and especially to Pamela A. Rooks, Professor of English at Francis Marion University, who kindly read this book in manuscript and made valuable suggestions.

As for the letters themselves, they exist today only because of the determined efforts of six people to preserve them from destruction. The authors' debt to those persons is enormous: to Oren Bradley Bounds, who made his way into the wreckage of Emily's home in Bay St. Louis after Hurricane Katrina and filled several large trash bags with quantities of soggy letters left behind by looters who saw no value in them, among them the handful written by Arlette, her father, and her brother Georges that are printed in this volume; to Madame ———, the late Jacques Baron's granddaughter and heir who, in an act of great empathy and *gentillesse* to two Americans she had never met, acceded to their request and ordered that the totality of Emily's letters to Arlette as well as the family photographs and newspaper clippings they contained be set aside and returned, rather than consigned to the trash in the course of preparing Arlette and Jacques Baron's home for an estate sale; to Yvan Carlassare, director of the Etude Généalogique Carlassare in Chambéry, France, who, as probate officer in charge of those proceedings, undertook with diligence and personal care to see to it that his client's orders were carried out; to Georges Delattre, who for four years made it his mission to oversee the rescue and retrieval of Emily's letters and photographs, perceiving in that task not only the opportunity to give an inestimable gift to his American cousins but also the duty to fulfill a loving promise he had made to his sister before her death; to Georges's wife Jeannine, who spent many days painstakingly sorting and dating Emily's materials, arranging them in chronological order, and packing them carefully for mailing; and especially to Arlette herself, who saved every letter, every photo, and every clipping that Emily had ever sent her throughout their sixty-year correspondence and who, though stricken with incurable and inexorably advancing illness, devoted the last months of her life to organizing the entire collection for its return to Emily after the loss of her home to Hurricane Katrina.

E. H. de M. and E. L. de M.

Note on Translations

All letters contained in this book are presented in English. Passages originally written in French have been translated into accurate, idiomatic English and (except for incidental phrases) are printed in italics.

"In this way, at least I can restore your past!"

Arlette Delattre Baron

I

In the Beginning

Like many family stories, this one could have several equally valid starting points—in 1854, for example, when Ludovic Adrien de Montluzin, a scholarly young journalist in Paris, became so opposed to the new regime of Napoleon III that he took his wife and children by sailing vessel to America to live.

Or in 1889 when the family returned to France for one of their rare visits with their Delattre relatives near Paris. It was then that Georges Delattre and Corinne de Montluzin, both in their 'teens, fell in love, though they realized that marriage would be out of the question for them. They were cousins, both from families with traditional views of blood relationships, and their romance would have to end when she and her family returned to America. Georges, who accompanied them to the train station on that day, wrote to Corinne of his grief when he saw her "dear little head" disappear into the departing crowd, and he told her that though they both might marry others, he would always love her *"quand-même"*—"anyway."

Georges did indeed marry and have a family, and Corinne was twice a widow. However, in their sporadic correspondence over several decades, *"quand-même"* became a code word for them. After Corinne's death in 1945 a handful of

Christmas cards would be found among her effects, each bearing the enigmatic (to other eyes) signature "*Quand-même.*"

Georges's last letter to her, written from Le Perreux, the small town on the outskirts of Paris where he owned a lithography business and was serving as deputy mayor, was dated May 4, 1940, one week before Nazi armies invaded France. *"I go back in my mind some 25 years on writing to you today,"* he told Corinne, *"because we were also then at war with our eternal enemy Germany, and now again an ambitious and bloodthirsty madman unleashes ruin and grief across Europe."* France had not yet been attacked, but he knew that the inevitable would come. *"We do not doubt here the final result, that is to say the punishment of Hitler and his bunch of gangsters, but in the meantime we must undergo the distresses of a state of war."* Turning to personal matters, he added:

> *In my last letter I remember I had sent you photos of my wife and children— Maurice, the eldest, is now 18 1/2 years old, Arlette 11 1/2, and Georges is 8. Maurice is a brilliant student who is about to take the second part of his baccalaureate. Arlette is already a beautiful young girl, first in her school. As for Jojo, he's a handsome little man who for the moment has no pretensions as a student. In short, I regret that the distance that separates us does not permit you to know their mother and the children. As for me, I am always busy because of the mobilization of all the volunteers [. . .]. But confidence is mounting in our country, and we are waiting for better days. I hope that our cause is well defended in the United States, which knows how to appreciate the desire for peace of the French people, who have done everything to avoid the war.*

Urging Corinne to write and sending her *"the friendly greetings of my wife and the children [. . .], with my best memories and my affectionate kisses,"* he closed his letter with the familiar *"T.Q.M."—"toujours quand-même."*

After that, there was no communication from the family in France, and Ludovic de Montluzin's descendants in America witnessed from afar, through radio broadcasts, newspaper accounts, and Fox Movietone newsreels, a succession of indelible images of events unfolding in the mother country: the surrender of France to Hitler in the railroad car in the clearing in the forest at Compiègne, Nazi soldiers parading in triumph down the Champs-Élysées as crowds of silent French onlookers wept, the heart-stopping assault on the beaches on D-Day, the Paris uprising against the German Occupation, and finally American and Free-French liberators streaming past the Arch of Triumph to the cheers of thousands of Parisians.

Perhaps, therefore, the real beginning of this family story should be in 1945, when the Nazi devastation and occupation of France had finally ended.

Ever since 1874 the American de Montluzins had lived in the Mississippi Coast resort town of Bay St. Louis built on a bluff beside a two-mile-wide bay. There Ludovic de Montluzin, a chemist as well as a journalist, had established an apothecary shop, the fifth in the state. At the end of World War II his son René, then seventy-nine years old, and his son, René, Jr., were the pharmacists and proprietors of the shop, by that time expanded into a full-scale drugstore overlooking the bay.

It was a white frame building, old-fashioned even in 1945, with its fourteen-foot ceilings, rounded glass display cases, rose marble soda fountain, black-and-white tiled floor, and frosted glass partition separating the customers from the inner sanctum of the prescription area, where the topmost shelves still bore large apothecary jars with crystal stoppers and gold-edged labels proclaiming their contents in bold, upper-case Latin—QUERCUS ALBA, HUMULUS, ACACIA, CORNU CERVIS,[1] etc.

Behind the shelves of drugs and the counter for prescription scales, mortars, pestles, and graduated beakers was the real nerve center of this family enterprise, its office. Here along one wall were bookcases filled with pharmacopoeias and drug journals. Mounted on another was the telephone, with

---

[1] White oak, hops, gum arabic, and deer horn, respectively

one of the earliest numbers in town: 23. In a corner stood a heavy black iron safe, and in the center were comfortable chairs grouped around a large round table, a perfect place for snatching quick meals, making out monthly bills, and counting the day's cash receipts every night after closing time. The entire building rested on creosoted pilings driven deep into the sand below. Its double front doors opened directly onto the sidewalk at the bluff's edge, and its back porch looked down toward the beach and the railroad bridge crossing the bay. To the family it was an extension of their nearby home.

One day in November 1945 the mayor of Bay St. Louis walked into the office, an envelope in his hand and undisguised curiosity on his face.

"Good morning, Mr. René! Here's a letter from France that came this morning addressed simply 'To the Mayor of Bay St. Louis, Mississippi, U.S.A.,'" he announced. "It enclosed this other letter along with a note asking me to deliver it if anyone named de Montluzin still lives here. So here it is!"

The excitement in the office was electric. At that moment all four of the 1945 family were there: René, Sr., and his wife Venie; René, Jr., just back from four years' military service as chief pharmacist in the Coast Guard Academy hospital in New London, Connecticut; and I, his wife Emily, who had returned with him from war work in Connecticut also, mine at the Electric Boat Company submarine yard in nearby Groton. René, Sr., ever an emotional man, silently handed the letter to his son to open.

The writer introduced herself. She was Arlette Delattre, sixteen years old, and she told us in good English that she wanted to notify the de Montluzin family in America that their Delattre relatives in France had survived the Nazi Occupation. Her father Georges, she said, was reestablishing his printing business, and her older brother Maurice was helping him there. She and her younger brother Georges ("Jojo") were at home with their mother Camille. She reported that their home in Le Perreux had been bombed but that they, the five Delattres, were alive and safe.

An immediate reply to Arlette's astounding letter was our top priority, and René, Sr., at once began planning what he would write, as head of the family in America, to his cousin Georges, whom he had last seen so long ago. Meanwhile, an even more pressing concern to all of us was sending packages of food to the Delattres, because we knew from news reports that many people in the Nazi-devastated countries of Europe were on the point of starvation and were unable to obtain even basic necessities. We had also heard that there were postal regulations about the size and weight of such parcels, and we all began to talk at once. René, always practical, thought immediately of cans of Spam.

"They'll need meat! That's essential!" he insisted.

My own idea was numerous packets of dehydrated soups, which would weigh practically nothing and which could be stuffed around other items in lieu of excelsior. René's mother, Venie, a superb chef, thought of flour, baking soda, and rice. (Arlette would tell us later that her mother had burst into tears at the sight of the two-pound bag of rice, the first she had seen in years.)

"Send coffee and cocoa," said his father.

"And sugar," added René.

"No, sugar's rationed over here," Venie mused. "But we could send a can of molasses instead."

"And let's put in a few Hershey bars," I exclaimed, "and some packs of gum for Jojo!"

Mentally I decided to include one additional small item as a present for Arlette herself, a little something extra—*lagniappe* in the New Orleans Creole tradition. Thinking of the bleakness of the five years of Nazi occupation and the gray sameness of a daily life ruled by grinding oppression and the dictates of bare necessity, I determined to add one personal gift, a lipstick. She would tell us later that it was the first she had ever owned.

As the excited planning continued, I started immediately to turn over in my mind what I would say in my own first letter to Arlette, this newly discovered young cousin who wrote so fluently and engagingly. I enjoyed writing and had taught French in our local high school before the war; I resolved that I would become the family scribe. What should I say, I thought, after expressing our joy that she and all of her family were safe? How could I best describe all four of us, our home, our town? Encapsulate the major events of our own lives, until recently so dominated by the war, just as theirs had been? I should enclose snapshots, I knew, but which ones? René in his uniform, certainly; an informal one of myself in a suit I liked; a photograph or two of his parents, perhaps posed, I considered rapidly, in front of the drugstore where they spent so much of their time.

I sat down at the table, put my French dictionary beside me, unscrewed my fountain pen, and wrote for the first time:

"Dearest Arlette...."

A new chapter in the lives of two families, an ocean apart, had begun.

II

Two Home Fronts
1945-1948

December 12, 1945

Dearest Arlette,

What excitement at our house this morning when your letter and M. Delattre's arrived![1] *I can't tell you with what pleasure and interest we read them. We have talked about them all day long and from time to time have looked again at the charming photos included. It's a great pleasure to make your acquaintance by means of these photos, and we're in high hopes of receiving others as soon as it's possible. We think that Georges, Jr., resembles my husband René, Jr., when he was twelve or thirteen years old.*

Before I write more, I want to say that I hope you will pardon all the errors in this letter—and there are a lot, I'm sure! I studied French, and I can read it without difficulty, but I haven't often had the occasion to write it; consequently I cannot do so well. But your usage of English, Arlette, is superb! I wish I could write French that well.[2]

---

[1] Arlette's letter described here, enclosing her father's as well as photos, was her second written to the de Montluzins. Emily's reply of December 12 was her first, René, Sr., having already written a month earlier to Georges Delattre in the name of the family to pledge all possible assistance.

[2] Emily's grammar and spelling were virtually flawless, but the rules of *politesse* had to be observed with the usual diplomatic formula of paying the other party the compliment of linguistic superiority, merited or not.

8

We are very sorry to learn from M. Delattre's letter that the situation in France is still so difficult, and we assure you of our great desire and pleasure in helping you in any way possible. We have already sent six packages, two about November 20 containing foodstuffs, meat, and cigarettes, and the other three [an error for four], *sent later, containing soap and woolen clothes. I must explain to you that there are postal regulations here: Each package can weigh no more than eleven pounds, each package must conform to specified dimensions, and each week only <u>one</u> package may be sent to the same person. This is why we have had to send many small packages and address them to various members of the family, although they are for everyone. I sent you one package, Arlette, without knowing your height and your size, and I am afraid that the clothes may not fit very well. However, I hope that in some way you can make use of them. From now on we'll try to do better!*

And now, because there is much more I want to say, and because you know English so well, Arlette, I shall continue in English, with a phrase now and then *en français* if the words come easily to me.

We are so glad that M. Delattre told us just what things you would like to have us send in our packages. It must be very hard not to have real soap to use, and *we'll send a lot of it in the next package.* In the packages addressed to you, we included two bars of mild facial soap, some spools of thread, some needles, and a lipstick, because we had heard that all these things are difficult to obtain—and now we wish that we had sent more soap than we did. Perhaps you do not need the needles, thread, and lipstick at all—but we took a chance on that. Next week, when the post office will accept two more packages, we shall send soap, candy, chocolate, canned meat, and some other warm clothing, including something especially for Georges, Jr., which we hope will fit him. You do not know, Arlette, how <u>very</u> <u>glad</u> we are to be able to help, even in this small way. Here in America we are so lucky to have an abundance of almost everything, although meat is not plentiful, sugar is still rationed very strictly, and new clothing is expensive and not of a good quality. However, we realize how fortunate our country is, and the average man on the street is eager to help any other country ravaged by the terrible war we have all experienced. Of course,

America was not damaged by bombs (as your beautiful home was! How terrible that must have been!) and our people were never hungry or persecuted by an enemy—but we gave many men, and in every town there are families saddened by the loss of a son, a brother, a husband, or a sweetheart. I do not know how people in Europe had the strength to survive these past years of war and terror. What courage and faith all of you must have had! What wonderful people you must be! We read many reports of the work of the F.F.I.[3] and were thrilled every time by their bravery and cleverness.

While I am on the subject of the war, I want to say that over here everyone is <u>angry</u> and <u>horrified</u> to read in the newspapers that many American soldiers now in France—especially in Le Havre—are acting so badly, attacking French girls, robbing French stores, and making French people think that Americans are almost as bad as the Germans! We are so <u>ashamed</u> of those soldiers, and our magazines and newspapers are urging their officers to punish them severely. I suppose in every country there are low-class, bad men, and many of ours must be in our army and navy. It grieves us to think that instead of making friends for America, they are only adding to the troubles you have had before. We are glad you told us that you have met some G.I.'s with <u>good</u> manners, and we hope you will judge America by <u>them</u>.

All of us enjoyed your description of V-E Day in Paris. It must have been wonderful! It is strange to think that you have seen General Eisenhower, and we never have. We like him very much too, and we have admired General de Gaulle for years. His determination and courage, especially during those dark days when he fought from England, were inspiring to the whole world. Just before V-E Day Mr. de Montluzin ordered a store in New Orleans to make, especially for him, five big new flags—French, English, Russian, Chinese, and American—and on V-E Day he had the Tricolor, the Union Jack, and the Stars and Stripes flying in front of his drugstore![4] It was so thrilling to read about the liberation of Paris

---

[3] *Forces Françaises de l'Intérieur* (French Forces of the Interior), the designation adopted by the French Resistance in 1944.

[4] Like René, Sr., Georges Delattre had made his own preparations for the victory he believed was approaching. Realizing that jubilant crowds in Paris would want to celebrate with flags when the

that we could not keep from crying a little for happiness. We hope to come to France, after a year or two, for a holiday. It is Mr. de Montluzin's dearest wish to visit France again. It will be fun for all of us to meet each other, won't it? We hope that all of you can some day come over and visit us in America— That would be wonderful.
Well, Arlette, this letter is becoming very long, isn't it? Mr. de Montluzin will reply soon to M. Delattre's charming letter, which we all enjoyed so much— and I must leave something for him to say. We thank you for your expressions of sympathy over the death of Aunt Corinne,[5] and we hope to hear from you again soon. Please give our greetings to M. and Mme Delattre, Maurice, Georges, and M. René.[6] We shall be thinking of all of you at Christmas and on New Year's Day!

Affectionately,
Emily de Montluzin

* * * * *

Bay Saint Louis, Miss.
January 28, 1946

Dearest Arlette,

I am so sorry that three weeks have passed without my being able to reply to your long letter, which we were all so happy to receive. I wanted to write you much sooner, but our house has been <u>like a hospital</u> since Christmas, with every

---

German surrender finally came, he astutely set the lithograph machines in his printing business to work, turning out a multitude of improvised paper Tricolors, Stars and Stripes, and Union Jacks. One large sample of each of the three flags remains in the possession of his son, Georges Delattre, Jr. "Jojo," as he was then called, was not so fortunate in his own efforts to celebrate the first Bastille Day after the war in Europe ended. As he wrote in English on July 16, 2009, "One of my first Bastille day memories is the first one after the Libération, it was in 1945, I was 13 and full of patriotic feelings, I wanted to join the march in Le Perreux, so, I took a bean stake in our garden at the end of which I fixed a blue-white-red lit chinese lantern and began to walk behind the veterans. They judged that initiative of bad taste and they threw me out, nearly kicking me. I felt that as a big injustice, I never forgot it."

[5] Corinne de Montluzin Lewis had died on March 22, 1945, in her seventy-fifth year.

[6] René Delattre, brother of Georges Delattre, Sr.

one of us sick at one time or another with bad colds. My mother and brother, who live in Texas, were spending the Christmas holidays with us, and they developed colds also—so at least one of us has been in bed taking medicine ever since Christmas Day. At present, it is René's time—he is in bed now reading a magazine while I am writing. It is very unusual for any of us to be ill, but for the last two months our weather has been very changeable—warm one day and quite cold the next—so that almost everybody in town has been sneezing and coughing.[7] But now all of us here at home are feeling well again, except René, and I believe that by tomorrow he will be all right too.

We were glad to know that you were having a happy Christmas, and it was fun to think that while the bells of your churches were ringing on Christmas Eve, you could hear over your radio the bells on Broadway! René and I spent the last three years in New London, a town in the state of Connecticut which was only three hours by train from New York City, so very often we went to New York to spend a few days and have fun. We saw several good plays on Broadway, and we enjoyed going to concerts, museums, French restaurants, and to Radio City Music Hall, the most beautiful building I have ever seen. (By the way, in one of the French restaurants there we tasted our first *bouillabaisse*, which we thought was delicious. In those restaurants one hears almost no English spoken, and the food is usually superbly prepared.)

I did not tell you much about any of us in my first letter, so I shall try to do so briefly in this one. When I finished school—at the University of Mississippi— I taught English, Latin, and a little Spanish in a small town in central Mississippi and then came down here to the coast to teach in Bay Saint Louis. Four days after I arrived here, a new friend took me into the de Montluzin Drug Store—and there I met René! All that year, 1941, he and I had many good times, going to football games and dancing and going sightseeing in New Orleans—even dressing as Pierrot and Pierrette and taking part in the Mardi Gras celebrations in New Orleans. That winter we became engaged to be married, and on the very afternoon

---

[7] The weakening of immune systems from the stress of war, coupled with the ease of contagion resulting from the movements of numbers of demobilized servicemen, even in a town as small as Bay St. Louis, could have been factors in the widespread outbreak of illness Emily describes.

the Japanese attacked Pearl Harbor, he was giving me my engagement ring. We had planned to have a honeymoon in Mexico, but he volunteered for service in the Coast Guard instead, and we postponed our wedding. He was sent to Connecticut, where he was in charge of the pharmacy in a big hospital for the rest of the war,[8] and I went to New Orleans as a translator of French and Spanish in the [newly established postal] censorship bureau there. However, in October, 1942, we decided not to wait any longer to be married, and in November René obtained ten days' leave in order to come home to be married. We had a beautiful wedding in the small church here in Bay Saint Louis where he had been christened, and we hurried back to Connecticut instead of to Mexico! We have no children yet—last summer we lost little twin baby boys—but we try not to think about our terrible disappointment and sorrow, and we hope we will yet be blessed with a family. As for the way we look, René has very blue eyes and wavy black hair, touched with a little gray, and he's not quite six feet tall. My eyes and hair are brown, and I'm five-and-a-half feet tall. René plays a violin, and we both like music, reading, movies, and swimming. René is a good tennis player, too. Do you enjoy swimming and tennis? I think we shall have a wonderful time when we meet each other! I know I would enjoy the European practice of bicycle-riding. That must be not only fun but good for one's figure.

As for René's mother and father, I believe I told you that Mr. de Montluzin was eighty years old in December and is still in the best of health. He is very jolly, always joking and teasing the young girls who come into the drugstore. He is very generous, too, and does much good that no one ever knows about.[9] Mrs. de Montluzin is the kindest, sweetest mother you can imagine. I am very lucky to have such a *belle-mère*! She's an excellent cook, too, and most of our food is prepared in the French way.

We are mailing you tomorrow a copy of a journal printed by the small newspaper office of our town on the occasion of the newpaper's fiftieth

---

[8] He served as chief pharmacist at the Coast Guard Academy hospital in New London, Connecticut, 1942-45.

[9] He extended credit to customers who could not pay their drug bills, and, when he saw the need, he secretly left bags of groceries at the doors of families in financial distress.

anniversary. The journal shows pictures of Bay Saint Louis taken many years ago (when the town was only a village) and pictures of many of the older citizens, dead for years, who helped to build the town. Mr. de Montluzin thought that M. Delattre especially would enjoy seeing the photographs of some of the de Montluzin family and reading the articles about them. The newspaper office is next door to our home, and its editor, who is now dead, was one of our friends.

I had wanted to write a lot in French this time, but my letter is nearly finished and I have written only in English! (To be truthful, Arlette, you write English so perfectly that I am ashamed of my efforts in French. In fact, there's a French dictionary here on the table right now!)

We hope that the little packages that we have sent have begun to arrive in good condition. About three weeks ago we sent the seventh, a box of soap and foodstuffs including some chocolate, some Hershey bars, and some packs of gum. When we are sure that the packages are reaching you, we want to send others. Perhaps we will soon receive a letter from you with the good news.

You said that you have read The Rains Came. *I have not read it, but I saw the movie with Tyrone Power, I believe, and Myrna Loy. It was very good, I thought. Like you, I really like Robert Taylor, Charles Boyer, Irene Dunne, and Merle Oberon, also Ingrid Bergman, Greer Garson, Clark Gable, and Paul Muni. I hope that you will see* Gone With the Wind *and* Rebecca. *We thought that they were excellent. One of the best movies that we've seen recently was* A Song to Remember, *with Merle Oberon, Paul Muni, and a new young actor, Cornel Wilde. It was in "technicolor," and the subject was the life and music of Chopin. I hope that soon you will be able to see it. The music was marvelous, especially the Polonaise.*

I must stop! I'm writing entirely too long a letter, I'm afraid. Thank you very much for your snapshot, which we all think is delightful. You certainly have lovely hair, Arlette. We have noticed it in all three of your pictures. If I can find any other pictures tonight that are good of us, I'll enclose some. We haven't taken any recently.

Please give our respects to all your family, and when you write, please tell us more about Cousin René. Mr. de Montluzin remembers especially how well he fought in the other war and is eager to hear more about him. I hope that Georges, Jr., will write me that letter you mentioned. I am looking forward to receiving it. And I hope, too, that soon I shall receive another letter from you, *ma chère* Arlette, <u>*as long as this one*</u>!

With much love,
Emily

P.S. Did you have a happy birthday? We were all thinking of you on that day.

[Editorial note:
Emily de Montluzin's laconic reference in the preceding letter to her work in the postal censorship bureau in New Orleans omits volumes, perhaps from ingrained wartime habits of not divulging military secrets.

Emily had graduated with honors from the University of Mississippi at the age of nineteen with a major in English, minors in French, Spanish, and Latin, and a license to teach in all four fields. At her late father's advice, she had taken a Civil Service examination in French and Spanish, obtaining certification as a translator of those languages to qualify herself for possible employment with the Department of State. Her plan for dual career paths was a prudent one in the depths of the Great Depression, when teachers were, in the denigrating parlance of the educational bureaucracy, "a dime a dozen." She did secure a teaching post late that summer at Yokona High School near Oxford, in what would later become known as "Faulkner Country." Her certification in languages would meanwhile remain on file with the Civil Service, dormant until December 7, 1941, when the Japanese attack on Pearl Harbor suddenly made it of prime relevance.

Several days after Pearl Harbor, FBI agents arrived at Bay High School in Bay St. Louis, Mississippi, where Emily was then teaching, called her out of her English class, and informed her that her country needed her more than her school did. They told her that postal censorship stations were being established in every port city in America to read all incoming and outgoing mail and that her services as a qualified translator of French and Spanish were required for the war effort.

Emily was assigned to the censorship bureau newly established on the second floor of the Federal Building on Lafayette Square in New Orleans, and her task, along with that of her coworkers, was to slit open each letter, scrutinize its contents, excise with a razor blade any portion that might be of use to the enemy (even inadvertent remarks from soldiers' families about troop deployments, the sight of freight trains loaded with tanks, etc.), and reseal the envelopes with gummed stickers bearing the censors' designated numbers. (Emily's number was 1956.) Her assignment was to read not only French and Spanish mail but also letters written in English if time permitted. Censors were warned to keep a vigilant watch for any letters that betrayed, by unidiomatic phrasing or convoluted syntax, the possible use of code and to reroute those letters to Washington, D.C., for examination by expert code-breakers. Such was the deluge of possibly suspicious letters sent to Washington that officials in the national Censorship Bureau decided to select small numbers of employees in each postal censorship station for training in codes and ciphers in order to perform a preliminary screening of suspect mail. Emily was one of the readers so designated in the New Orleans bureau.

One day in the spring of 1942, when there happened to be a dearth of French and Spanish mail, Emily chose at random a letter from the pile of English-language mail dumped unceremoniously in the center of her table. The writer's odd phraseology and slightly irregular syntax immediately aroused her suspicion; and, following the code-and-cipher protocol she had been taught, she copied the letter onto graph paper, one letter per square, and proceeded to examine the patterns of letters with the aid of a ruler, checking forwards and backwards; vertically, horizontally, and diagonally; every third letter, fifth letter, seventh letter, eleventh letter, etc. The possible permutations were legion. Failing to perceive any recognizable pattern, she went home to her boarding house at the end of the day with nothing to show for her efforts but a severe headache from eyestrain. Her second day's work on the letter produced no results except for another headache, but she knew instinctively that there was something suspicious about that letter. Resolving that if, at the end of the third day, she still could achieve no breakthrough, she would send the letter on to Washington to wait its turn for more expert analysis, she set to work again. That day, after several more hours with the graph paper and ruler, the message, as she described it later, "leaped off the page." It was a plot to blow up a lock in the Panama Canal.

She rushed to her supervisor's desk and showed him the letter; and a quick telephone call from him to the FBI offices on the third floor of the Federal Building summoned two agents, who burst into the room, snatched up the letter, and literally ran out the door.

The Panama Canal was not destroyed; the war effort in the Pacific was not impeded. Emily was to learn only decades later of the arrest in 1942 and subsequent conviction in the federal district court in the Canal Zone of several enemy operatives for plotting to blow up a lock in the Panama Canal. (Edit.)]

* * * * *

Bay Saint Louis, Miss.
April 11, 1946

My dear Arlette,

I remember that I began my last letter expressing my apologies to you, and now I have to repeat them! We have received three letters from you, Maurice, and M. Delattre since I wrote to you, and I can't tell you how ashamed I am. But it seems that, since René and I came home in November, I have become a member of so many organizations and clubs that now I realize that I don't have time for my own affairs! I think I'll have to drop out of some of them, but we are so happy to find ourselves at home again that it's a pleasure to be with our friends in almost all of the societies that have been formed here. The principal thing that demands so much attention now is "Le Petit Théâtre," which has just been organized here and of which René, Mme de Montluzin, and I are enthusiastic members. I am one of the members of the committee which reads a lot of plays and decides the ones which will be presented, and René is president of the committee which furnishes the music at each performance. (He plays the violin—did I tell you that before?) We presented the first play three weeks ago—The Twelve Pound Look by Sir James M. Barrie—and I played the role of "Emmy." Perhaps you can find the book and read it. There are about 200 members of the Little Theater already, and last week someone gave us an old red building which we intend to repair and make into a <u>real</u> theater! Already we have had lots of fun, and we've made several new friends whom we are glad to know. We are presenting another one-act play next week and a three-act comedy next month, but I am not in either of them. That's good, for now I will have more time to write my letters [. . .].

Mr. de Montluzin asks me to beg your father to forgive him for waiting so long to write, but the truth is that he is doing enough work for <u>two</u> men every day, and for the last few months he hasn't had any time at all for anything else. He intends to write when he can and he appreciates your father's charming letters very much. All of us are so interested in M. Delattre's paintings, and we can hardly wait to receive the one he plans to send us! I am very fond of landscapes, and I know the banks of the Marne are beautiful. We are all looking forward to seeing them in his painting.[10]

I believe that by this time you must have received two more packages from us—the ones containing food and six shirts. It is almost impossible to buy men's clothing now, because ever since the war ended there have been so many <u>strikes</u> in clothing factories.[11] Isn't it disgusting and foolish? Everything is of bad quality, too. René had many shirts left from prewar times, so he sent the six you found in the two packages. We are sorry they are not new ones, but the stores are almost bare of men's things. Maybe in a few months the situation will be better. Two days ago we sent two more packages, and we have still two others ready to send next week. I wish we could send larger boxes and more of them at once, but the postal regulations will not allow more than 11 pounds per box and <u>one</u> <u>box</u> <u>per</u> <u>week</u>. We manage to send <u>two</u> boxes at one time, however, by using different names of <u>your</u> family as the <u>addressee</u> and by saying that different members of <u>our</u> family are sending the boxes. I am sure you wondered at first why a box addressed to <u>Maurice</u>, perhaps, might contain articles evidently meant for <u>you</u> or your <u>mother</u>. But really every box is meant for every one of you, and

---

[10] Georges Delattre, an amateur painter of great ability, was eager to reciprocate for all of the packages of food and clothing his American cousins were sending to his family. Unable to obtain canvas readily in wartime or postwar France, he sometimes painted on wood as the best possible substitute available to him. Over the course of the next several years he sent the landscape mentioned above (a view of a viaduct over the Marne, painted near his home in Le Perreux shortly before its destruction by the retreating German forces), a landscape of Notre Dame at sunset as seen from the banks of the Seine, a still-life of hydrangeas, and portraits of René de Montluzin, Sr., and his wife Venie, and of René de Montluzin and his wife Emily.

[11] Strikes in clothing factories were only a small part of the labor troubles in the immediate postwar epoch. "Labor unions, free of their wartime pledges not to strike, called for 'catch-up' pay hikes," David McCullough notes, and, as a result, "[s]trikes broke out in nearly every industry." (David McCullough, *Truman* [New York: Simon & Schuster, 1992], 470.) On November 21, 1945, the automobile workers' strike against General Motors had begun, and in January 1946 the Steel Workers' Union had shut down steel mills nationwide. Ten days before Emily wrote her letter to Arlette, John L. Lewis's United Mine Workers had begun a crippling two-month strike against the soft coal mines. On May 21, 1946, Truman would seize the coal mines; and four days later, with the threat of a nationwide rail strike looming, he would go before Congress to ask for authority to draft striking train operators into the Army. The measure, which the House of Representatives passed in a vote of 306-13, would be defeated in the Senate; but by that time the rail strike was over. (Ibid., 480-81, 492-506.)

we hope Cousin René can use some of the things, too. We were sorry to hear of his rheumatism and his other misfortune— *C'est dommage*—

In the last two boxes there are two lightweight suits that René had before the war and that he cannot wear now, since he has gained some weight. A third suit is ready to go next week. It would be nice if Maurice, M. Delattre, and Cousin René were all the same size so that each one could have one of the suits. We were shocked to learn that a new suit in France costs so much! These are not new, but we hope they can be used to advantage for everyday wear. At any rate we hope they can be made to fit <u>one</u> of them. The linings of the coat sleeves are not good, but perhaps Mme Delattre can repair them. It is wonderful to think that she was a *première* [i.e., had a leading position in a dress shop] on the rue de la Paix! Every time I think of it I am thrilled! Please tell her, Arlette, that I have started learning to sew (a sewing class was organized among my friends two weeks ago)—and I wish she could be here to teach me how. By the way, since you said in your letter that you are going to the coast this summer, we put into one of the boxes a piece of cotton material which we thought Mme Delattre might make into a "play-suit" for you to wear on the beach. There's a piece of brown material for her, too, and a pair of brown shoes Mrs. de Montluzin is sending, which will probably be too large for either of you but which perhaps someone you know will be able to wear. For Georges, Jr., we put in a whole box of chewing gum, but we hope he will divide some of the packages of gum with the rest of you!

One of our friends here has a son who is stationed at Frankfurt and who often comes to Paris, and she sent him the address of your family about two weeks ago, hoping that when he goes to Paris again, he will be able to call on you. His name is Lt. Walter James Phillips, and he is a very nice young man whom we believe all of you would like to meet.

We talk all the time about our own proposed trip to Paris. We want so much to come and to have you visit us here in America! Paris is like a wonderful dream to me, and when you speak of theatres, dancing, museums, etc., Arlette, I can hardly wait to come. Yes, I like dancing very much, and so does René. Your canoe trips on the Marne sound like fun, too. We will teach you more American songs when we come, and I'll try to talk with you in Spanish. My Spanish isn't very good, though.

I must stop all my chatting here. All the family joins me in sending you as well as M. and Mme Delattre, Maurice, Georges, and Cousin René our most affectionate thoughts. Write us soon, and forgive me for my long delay. I won't do it again!

Much love always,
Emily

* * * * *

Tuesday, April 23 [1946]

Dearest Arlette,

[Emily begins her letter with apologies for her long delay in writing.] [. . .]

We enjoyed your letter very much. In fact, we think that you, your father, and Maurice ought to be <u>writers</u> <u>by</u> <u>profession</u>, since you do it so well! All three of you write such interesting letters that we read them over and over again, whenever we receive one. The pictures came too, and we have looked at every one of them so often that I believe we have memorized every feature and would know all of you immediately if we met you unexpectedly on the street one day! But why was there no picture of you, Arlette? We missed you! We think "Jo-jo" and Maurice extremely handsome, M. Delattre most distinguished, and your sweet mother a charming lady whose laughter and good sense of humor must make your home a happy one! We had to laugh at the snapshot of your mother, taken at such a moment! Jo-jo is <u>very</u> <u>much</u> like René, as you said you noticed too, from René's pictures. We are all grateful to you for sending the photographs, for they are so excellent that I know you must have hated to part with them. I hope that you have copies.

I am enclosing a few pictures in this letter, though they are not very recent ones.[12] We have difficulty getting film now, but the situation is improving, and I hope we can send new photos soon. The picture of me was an extra one I had kept after the New Orleans newspapers announced my approaching marriage in 1942.

We are glad the 8th and 9th packages reached you, but we are distressed to think that the coffee had been removed. Was there a large can of syrup in that box? We thought that it would be good to have if there is a scarcity of sugar. From now on I think that I shall write you exactly what we pack into each box so that you will know if anything is missing (though of course it would really do no good to know, would it?). As I wrote you, we sent the 10th and 11th boxes about two weeks ago, and yesterday I mailed the 12th and 13th. The last two contained a gray suit, shoes (probably too big for Mme Delattre, but maybe the right size for someone you may know), four bars of soap, a box of Hershey bars, brown dress material, rice, coffee, Spam, spaghetti, a can of spaghetti sauce, and a box of flour (to which you must add only water, and you will have delicious *pain d'épice*— "gingerbread," as we call it here). I hope all these arrive safely. We had to pack the trousers of the gray suit in one box and the coat in the other in order to make all the articles fit into the small space properly. I do wish the boxes could be larger and weigh more! Twice I have taken them to the post office only to find that they weighed 2 ounces more than 11 pounds, so I have carried them home again and removed perhaps one bar of soap or one can of sardines in order to bring the weight down enough. I really think those regulations are absurd, don't you?

By the way, Arlette, please tell me in your next letter which, of the things we send, you like best and need most—or tell me if there is something else we

---

[12] The photos of the four de Montluzins included a black-and-white snapshot of René in uniform, posed in front of the Coast Guard Academy hospital. He had inscribed it with these words: "My four years' service to my country was given voluntarily with the determined desire in my heart that one day the world would find itself at peace—and the honor and glory restored to France!" Some twenty years later, after returning from his long-awaited trip to France with Emily and their daughter Lorraine, René de Montluzin would write on September 5, 1966, "I live in America but my blood is French [. . .]."

might send that we have not thought about. I wish there were some way to send butter or oil, but it is impossible. You say that all of you are happy to receive the packages, but I believe that we are even happier to send them. We all hope that America will do all it can to help alleviate the food shortage in Europe this summer, because it seems so terrible to think that we have more than enough when others need food so badly. I am sure that Mr. Hoover's report[13] will be very valuable, and Mr. La Guardia[14] is a man who usually finds a way to have things done! I only hope our country's help will be given soon enough to do its utmost good.

You were right about our being in New Orleans while you were listening to the Carnival broadcast. René and I were on St. Charles Street that very minute! It is thrilling to think that you heard the music and singing. I hope we can take all of you to enjoy the Mardi Gras celebrations with us some day. I think you would like New Orleans very much; it is still a French city.

Do you play a card game called contract bridge, Arlette? It is very popular in America, and I'm sure it is played in France also. I belong to a group of eight girls who play together every Tuesday afternoon. All of us are married, and we talk about our husbands and our homes more than we play bridge! Each week we meet in the home of a different member of our little club, and we play from 1:30 until about 5:30. Sometimes we meet at night instead so that our husbands can join us. I like the game very much, though I'm not an expert player at all. However, summertime is almost here, and soon it will be much more fun to be outdoors. I wish we had a kayak like Maurice's new one! Already some people are swimming, and every night when the tide is low, we can ride along the beach and see many people with electric or gasoline torches wading in the shallow water and catching crabs and flounders. It is very easy to catch them—

---

[13] Herbert Hoover had been appointed by Truman in 1946 to a fact-finding mission to the Western zones of occupied Germany, a mission that led to the provision by the United States of food aid that supplied millions of meals to German schoolchildren.
[14] Fiorello H. LaGuardia served from April through December 1946 as Director General of the United Nations Relief and Rehabilitation Administration, overseeing a massive project not only to supply needed food and medical supplies but also to rebuild the infrastructure of war-ravaged Europe.

even children do it—and the torch lights moving against the blackness of the water make a very picturesque sight as one rides along. I believe M. Delattre might like to paint such a scene.

You mentioned seeing *Objective Burma*, Arlette. Yes, we saw that in New London and thought it was a wonderful picture. I agree with you about *The Rains Came*. I liked the book better, too. We see a great many movies, because René and I like to go to them, and since this is a small town, we cannot go to the theater. I've been reading about how gay the theater season in Paris is this year. Have you seen Claudine Cereda in *No, No, Nanette?*[15] Oh, by the way, we saw last night in the Movietone News several pictures of the terrible murderer Dr. Petiot[16] during his trial. Such a man <u>must</u> be insane; don't you think so? But I certainly hope his legal cleverness doesn't win a light sentence for him!

Please tell your mother that I have begun to take lessons in sewing. I'm making a simple seersucker dress now. (In case you don't know that word, it's the cotton material that does not require *repassage*. Is that the right word? We call it <u>ironing</u> or <u>pressing</u>.) I hope I can learn how to sew well. Do you like to sew, Arlette? When we visit you in France, perhaps Mme Delattre will teach me a few things herself! I wish she would. We talk all the time about our proposed visit—I wish we could be leaving tomorrow! All the plans you write me about make us impatient to start at once. I suppose it will have to be next year, though, when conditions for travel are better. You are all so kind to want us to come, and we <u>are</u> coming!

---

[15] The account Emily had read was "The Theater: Paris in the Spring," *Time*, April 15, 1946, 90-91, which reported (p. 90) that *No, No, Nanette* "was the smash hit of the season, grossing 210,000 francs ($1,763) a performance—a terrific take for present-day Paris." The review further noted that among the 52 plays (exclusive of musicals) presented in the resurgence of theatre in Paris in 1946 were Sartre's *Huis Clos* and T. S. Eliot's *Murder in the Cathedral*.

[16] Marcel André Henri Félix Petiot (1897-1946), doctor with dubious medical credentials and a long history of embezzlement, who preyed on Jews and others seeking to flee from France, charging exorbitant fees for helping them to "escape" and then murdering them, stealing their valuables, and disposing of their bodies by means of quicklime and his own basement stove. Convicted of over two dozen counts of homicide, he was guillotined on May 25, 1946. The *New York Times* gave extensive coverage to the trial and execution of the "Paris 'Bluebeard'"; see especially the issues of March 18, 1946, p. 2, col. 3; April 5, 1946, p. 11, cols. 2-4 (with photograph of Petiot and his legal counsel); April 6, 1946, p. 3, col. 6; May 25, 1946, p. 9, col. 2; and May 26, 1946, p. 5, cols. 2-3.

This time I've been lazy and have written only in English. Next time I'll do better, though. We hope to hear from Jojo and that you will write soon again. All our family send love to all of you, *y para ti, Arlette, todo el cariño de tu prima que te quiere,*

Emily

* * * * *

May 19, 1946

Ma chère Arlette,

This time I'm following your suggestion and writing only a note in order to give you Walter James Phillips's address without delay [. . .]. [Emily supplies Lt. Phillips' military address in Frankfurt and notes that he had recently been an observer at the Nuremberg War Crimes Tribunal. He would write to the Delattre family on July 7, 1946, that he regretted not having had "a more direct part in seeing that those criminals received their due."]

We are delighted to know that M. Delattre is in the process of working on our painting! We are looking forward to receiving it and hope that the difficulties of shipping it to us will not be too much trouble for him. It is so kind of him to want to paint a picture especially for us, and we are already very grateful to him.

I'm enclosing a few pictures showing play suits and other beach clothes being worn in the United States this summer. Next time I'll send more.

René and I received a long, interesting letter from Maurice this week, with several charming snapshots he had taken around Espalion. We are so glad he is so much better. Please tell him we enjoyed his letter very, very much and will write him soon to say so ourselves.

We are happy that you told us exactly what you need the most, Arlette. It happens that for the last three years it has been impossible even in America to buy sheets, since cloth has been used instead for uniforms, clothes, etc. But at the beginning of the war, when I knew I was soon to be married, I bought a dozen sheets, and Mrs. de M. has some she has never used either; so we can easily spare two sheets each for you, which we hope will help you out a little. I wish we could send more than 4, but it is still impossible to buy them. Maybe soon conditions will be better and we can get you some more. We are so happy to send these four and will mail them right away with all our love. Please don't even think about offering to pay us for anything we send, because it is one of our greatest pleasures. When we come to Paris, your wonderful hospitality and the sights of *La Belle France* will be more than enough payment! I'll write soon again. Thank you for the impressive snapshot you sent. *Recuerdos a toda la familia, y para ti abrazos y besitos de tu prima que tanto te quiere,*

Emily

P.S. In English, "une fossette" is "a dimple"—and I have two of them! When I was little, my mother used to say, "The fairies kissed you on both cheeks while you were asleep one night."

P.P.S. This morning, among the souvenirs of Mrs. Lewis,[17] we found the little card announcing your birth, Arlette!

* * * * *

Dallas, Texas
June 27, 1946

Dearest Arlette,

Your letter of June 2 arrived in Bay St. Louis two days before I left to visit my mother[18] *and brother in Dallas. I have been here for two weeks, and I have wanted every day to write to you and ask you to express to M. Delattre my great*

---

[17] The late Corinne de Montluzin Lewis

[18] Emily Gayden Hosmer, who in her mid-fifties had joined Emily and René de Montluzin in New London and taken a war job on the wet dock of the pipefitting department of the Electric Boat Company. Her assignment was to keep a record of each tool checked out by the pipe-fitters (many of whom were French Canadians who had moved to Connecticut seeking war work) and then to make an entry in her files when the tool was returned. She freely admitted that she did not know one wrench from another, and the French Canadians spoke very little English, so they simply pointed to each tool that they needed. She had accepted the job only after she had been assured that she could wear a skirt instead of trousers to work! Because hers was a blue-collar job, her salary was higher than her daughter Emily's, whose position as secretary to the shipyard manager was classified as white-collar.

gratitude for his intention to paint my portrait! Tell him, please, Arlette, that I am enchanted at the idea, and I cannot thank him enough. In fact, all the family is as happy as I am, and we will all be very proud to have an oil painting of me! (I think that I should not try to write French without a dictionary, since I have to think so long over each word, and even then I am sure I make many mistakes.)

I think your father is wonderfully kind to propose undertaking such a task, which I know will require many, many hours of his time, and I do not know how to tell him how grateful I shall be. When I left Bay St. Louis, I gave a picture to Mrs. de Montluzin to send to you, and I suppose that by this time it is on its way to France. It is like the photo in the New Orleans newspaper, but larger and in colors. Since it was made just before I married, I think that it is the one I should like to have copied in oils best of all. The colors in the picture are poorly applied, but they are right except for my hair. Please tell M. Delattre that in reality I have red-gold light in my hair, though in the picture it appears to be only dark brown. The blouse I am wearing is white, but if he would like to paint it some color, I think I look best in pale green or in gold. However, I wish that he would use his own good judgment about that. I shall be so happy to have his wonderful gift, which I shall treasure as long as I live and feel very, very proud to possess.

While we were looking for an extra copy of my picture to send to M. Delattre, we found among some of Aunt Corinne's things a photo of René which he had sent her while we were in New London, Connecticut. I have another copy of the same picture, and his mother has one, too; so we decided to send Aunt Corinne's copy to you, thinking that you might like to have it. It is a <u>very</u> good picture of René, though he is usually smiling and does not often look so serious. Mrs. de Montluzin said that she would send it at the same time she mailed my picture to your father.

I am sorry to have been compelled to wait almost three weeks to answer your charming letter, *ma chère Arlette,* but this is what happened: My mother came to Bay St. Louis to spend a week with us, the same week that your letter arrived, and since she was being entertained by several of our friends and since I was preparing to return with her to Dallas, I did not have enough time to sit down calmly and write as long a letter to you as I wanted to write. We left Bay St.

Louis on June 16th, and during the two weeks that I have been here, I have gone out so much that the time has flown away *dans un clin d'oeil* ["in the blink of an eye"]. (Isn't that the way to say it?) My mother and Harry[19] have showed me all the interesting sights in Dallas, and I have had a wonderful time. I am so sorry René could not come with me, but he is especially busy in the summertime. This fall we hope to go to Mexico [. . .].

[Emily describes the city of Dallas, its enormous population growth during World War II, its parks and outdoor stage for summer operettas, and its Neiman-Marcus department store, "generally considered to be finer than any other store in the United States, even in New York."]

We enjoyed your letter so much, Arlette, and are glad that the last packages arrived safely. We hope that Maurice and M. Delattre will be able to use the suits occasionally and are so glad they fit them well. Please, dear Arlette, do not worry about the cost of the articles nor about whether we are depriving ourselves. I can understand well how all of you must feel in this matter, but we know that the only reason we are more fortunate in our economic welfare in America than you are in France is because French people had to endure the German plague and we didn't. We respect your bravery and fortitude, and whatever we can do to help while France is regaining its former prosperity is only too little. As for repaying us, your hospitality when we come to France next year or the next will be a delightful payment! We are looking forward so much to that trip and talk about it all the time. It is truly a pleasure to us to send the few boxes we have sent, and we are delighted that they are of use to you. We mailed two other boxes containing sheets and some *denrées* [foodstuffs] about a month ago. Mr. de M. also asked us to include some toothbrushes, toothpaste, razor blades, and a razor, because someone recently returned from France had told him that those items are hard to obtain. We hope that you can use them too. Don't worry about the sheets, because we have plenty left. We have to apologize that two of

---

[19] Harry Gayden Hosmer, Emily de Montluzin's younger brother, who had recently resumed his prewar employment as an accountant in the Department of Agriculture. His wartime experience was in the Pacific Theater, on a ship, oddly enough for a sergeant in the Army Air Force.

them have been used one time and washed, but they are of strong material which will last a long time.

I'm glad that you saw *Thirty Seconds over Tokyo*, Arlette. I thought it was one of the best pictures I ever saw. I cried twice in it! Did you? I think the best one I've seen recently is *Leave Her to Heaven*, with Cornel Wilde and Gene Tierney. I hope it comes to Paris soon. Be sure to see it.

I must stop now and mail this. I am enclosing a letter to Maurice also. My mother and brother ask to be remembered to you and your family and they send all of you their very best regards. Have a wonderful time on your vacation, Arlette, and let us have another of your sweet letters soon! Everyone at home sends love to all of you.

All my love always,
Emily

*   *   *   *   *

Bay St. Louis
Sunday, Oct. 6th [1946]

Ma chère Arlette,

This time it is I who must make excuses. Your lovely letter arrived more than a month ago, and I've talked each day about writing to you, but a lot of things have happened to delay me. The principal thing was that the little son of our most beloved cousin died on August 3; and when your letter came, all the family was so overcome with grief that I could not calm down enough to reply to you. The little boy was only two years old, and he was his mother's and father's only child—and the terrible thing is that the doctors have no idea of the cause of his death.[20] *Olga and Dick (his mother and father) are very brave, but naturally their grief is crushing, and all the family is desolate as well.*

---

[20] Richard Drown, Jr., who had been in perfect health, died several days after receiving his diphtheria vaccination.

But, returning to your letter, Arlette, we were very happy and surprised to know that <u>good, sweet</u> M. Delattre has made a portrait of René also! He is very kind, really, and we are afraid that he's giving himself too much trouble. <u>One</u> portrait would have been a marvelous gift, and <u>two</u> are absolutely overwhelming! We will always be grateful to M. Delattre, and I wish I could express myself better in French [. . .]. We will await the arrival of the portraits with the greatest impatience, and when René and I build our house, the portraits will be the first things that will be seen there.

Tuesday, October 8th [1946]

Oh, Arlette! Today, before I could finish the letter I began writing to you on Sunday night, your letter written <u>only three days ago</u> arrived! We are so happy and pleased over the wonderful snapshots of our portraits, and we can hardly wait to see the portraits themselves [. . .] so that we can see them in color. We decided today that when they arrive, we shall have a party and invite all our friends to come to see them. If only all of you could come also! When you <u>do</u> come, however, we shall have another party [. . .].

[After more discussion of the paintings and of Arlette's recent vacation on the Riviera, Emily reverts to the trip to Paris she and the rest of the family hope to make.] It seems like a dream to think that maybe next summer we shall see all of you and many of the beautiful places in France. About a month ago I went to a large travel bureau in New Orleans to ask if it will be possible to travel to France <u>by boat</u> next summer. They said no, unless the boats that are being reconditioned for passenger service are ready sooner than they expect. However, they told me to inquire again in a few months, because the situation may be better then. Mr. de M. doesn't want to go to France by airplane, and René prefers a boat, too. They say that the pleasure of a sea voyage is one of the things they are hoping to enjoy. As for me, however, the principal thing is <u>arriving</u> in France, and perhaps I can persuade them to consider the airplane.

Please thank M. Delattre and Jojo (and Bikini![21]) for their snapshots. Your father is very distinguished and charming, Arlette! And Jojo's smile and the

---

[21] Georges, Jr.,'s cat

twinkle in his eye will surely win many friends for him. We had not realized that he is so tall. We are more convinced than ever that he resembles René very much. You asked about our Little Theater. It is growing very rapidly, and we are presenting a play every month. In August we presented two one-act plays on the same program, and I was the director of one play—Lord Dunsany's *A Night at an Inn.* The characters are seven men—no women—and I was the director. We worked very hard on the play, and we presented it for three nights. Everyone said it was good, and I really think myself that the actors performed well. The play is a terrifying drama, full of murders and off-stage screams. Perhaps you can find a copy of it to read. It is not a good play for reading, however, because it is the action and the dimly lighted stage that make the story effective. I am enclosing a program for you to see.

Our sewing class no longer exists. Our teacher has additional duties and could not find time for us any longer, but I intend to make a few things this fall. The bridge club still meets every Tuesday. I told the girls today about our portraits, and they are all excited and eager to see them.

Please thank M. Delattre, Arlette *chère*, for his kindness in offering to paint portraits of Mr. and Mrs. de M. also. They are very grateful, but they feel that he has already done so much for us that anything more would be an imposition. But they are deeply touched by his offer and wish to convey their appreciation to him.

I have seen all the movies you mentioned except *La Symphonie Pastorale.* I hope it will come soon. I especially liked *Madame Curie.* How much the world owes to her and to her husband! I shall wait until my next letter to talk more about movies and books. In this one, I want to be sure to say how interesting your new work sounds! I can imagine no more pleasant place to work than in a fashionable shop on the rue de la Paix or the Place Vendôme! Tell me more about it, Arlette, when you write again. I know you and Mme Delattre must have enjoyed the *Collection de Couturier.* I attended a showing of Northridge hats in New Orleans recently, and I saved a clipping from the newspaper to send to you. Some of the hats cost as much as $800 or $900! Everything is very expensive here too. I think it is chiefly because of labor strikes.

Arlette, we would like very much to know what things are still difficult to obtain in France, because we are eager to send more packages to you and we want to include in them the things you would really enjoy receiving. When you write again, will you tell me some things? Are soap, meats, candy, etc., still hard to obtain? Shirts are more plentiful now. Do M. Delattre and Maurice still find them difficult to buy? What about Jojo? Could you tell me his size in shirts too? And Mme Delattre and yourself? Please tell me, because it gives us the greatest pleasure to feel that we are able to help a little while France is recovering from the war.

I simply must stop! Please give our regards and love to all your family. We are hardly able to wait for the portraits and the landscape to arrive! Write me soon, Arlette. I love your letters!

All my love to you always,
Emily

* * * * *

Bay St. Louis, Miss.
October 30, 1946

Dearest Arlette,

[Emily begins her letter by reporting that the package with Georges Delattre's paintings, shipped weeks before, had not yet arrived and that she was "beginning to become a little anxious [. . .]."]

The second thing I wanted to tell you is that today we mailed two boxes to you, containing about the same kind of things we have sent before. We hope that they will still be useful, although of course we hope also that the situation in France is becoming better. Here, because of innumerable strikes and price regulations, many items are almost impossible to obtain. Sugar and oil and rice are some of the most difficult to find, but fortunately Mrs. de M. was able to get enough last week so that she sent some of each to Mme Delattre in these two packages. We also sent cigarettes, soap, Hershey bars, coffee, and flour, and a dress which my mother in Dallas sent me to send to Mme Delattre, hoping that she might find some use for it. My mother has never worn it, intending to keep it for this winter, but during the summer she gained almost ten pounds and now cannot wear it at all! We do not know whether materials for dresses are hard to obtain in France or not—here, all materials are extremely expensive and scarce. I was fortunate in finding a pretty piece of wool recently, and my dressmaker has just finished making a new suit for me. The suit has a gored skirt, a sleeveless vest, and a very lovely jacket. I am enclosing a sample of the material for you to see.

Speaking of how difficult it is to obtain everything, we hope that soon the situation will improve, because last week most of the government price controls were abolished.[22] We expect prices to rise for a few weeks, but when manufacturers begin to produce in large quantities again, competition will probably cause prices to fall. At least, that's what we hope.[23]

If possible, I am going to enclose in this letter the program of our last Little Theater play. It was Noel Coward's comedy, *Hay Fever*, and our biggest success. We presented it for five nights to capacity audiences.

Last Saturday René and I drove in to New Orleans with two friends of ours and had a wonderful time. In the afternoon we attended a big football game (about 50,000 spectators) and afterwards had a delicious dinner at a French restaurant called Arnaud's, which you must visit when you come here. That night we attended the opera *La Traviata*, which was beautiful, both in music and costumes. I wish all of you could have been with us!

We are all well, and everyone sends love to you and all the family. Please forgive my laziness in writing only in English! Next time I'll do better. Write us soon, Arlette, please!

Je t'aime,
Emily

---

[22] On October 14, 1946, price controls had been lifted from livestock and meat, and on November 9, 1946, all remaining price controls on commodities were abolished with the exception of those on sugar and rice.
[23] By the end of 1946 consumer prices had risen to 19.5% above their 1935-39 average. (F. H. Heller, ed., *Economics and the Truman Administration*, The Harry S. Truman Library Institute for National and International Affairs [Lawrence: Regents Press of Kansas, 1981], xvi.)

P.S. How do you like your new work? I hope it is pleasant and that you enjoy it.

* * * * *

                                              Bay St. Louis
                                              November 26, 1946

Dearest Arlette,

      Your letter of November 21st (which was written on our fourth wedding anniversary!) arrived today, and we enjoyed it so much. The portraits have not arrived yet, however, and now our impatience has grown so great that we can hardly wait from one day to the next to receive them! Surely they will come soon and will make our Christmas an especially happy one.

      Before I write any more, I must tell you some very bad news. Just a week ago Mrs. de Montluzin fell and broke her left hip! We took her in an ambulance to a hospital in New Orleans, so that a very good bone surgeon there could set her broken bones, and she is still in the hospital. This is what happened: She had been to the beauty parlor that afternoon, and when she left, it was beginning to rain and she was walking fast. The sidewalk was uneven, and she tripped and fell heavily. The doctor who X-rayed the injury here in Bay St. Louis advised us to take her immediately to New Orleans where a specialist might attend her. So that same night René, his father, and I rode in the ambulance with her the sixty miles to New Orleans through a terrible rainstorm. We took her to a hospital where her youngest sister is a nurse, and the doctor there made an incision in her leg and put a long metal <u>pin,</u> or <u>nail,</u> through the bones to hold them together! It is a modern method used during the war very successfully. Perhaps you have heard of it? She will be able to come home in about two weeks and can move about the house on crutches then. It is really wonderful, because, as you know, most people with broken hips have to spend many months in bed. The doctor says in about three or four months she will be perfectly well again.

      You can imagine how upset and anxious all of us have been this week. We miss her very much, of course. Another sister of hers (the grandmother of the little boy who died) has come to help us with cooking and housekeeping while she is away, and I don't know what we would do without her. We are very busy at the drugstore, too, because in America drugstores sell many gift articles which are in great demand at Christmas time.

Speaking of Christmas, Arlette, just before Mrs. de M.'s accident we sent two more boxes to all of you containing a few small Christmas gifts and "goodies" which we hope you will all enjoy. They were mailed on November 13th, exactly six weeks before Christmas Day, and I am praying that they will arrive in time for Christmas. It is terrible that you are without electricity two days a week! Oh, Arlette, please tell Jojo that I will try to find shirts for him as soon as possible. I am so glad to know his exact size. In the meantime, we hope he will like his Christmas present anyhow. I am sure M. Delattre will enjoy part of his, judging by what you said in your letter today!

I haven't been to the travel bureau again, but I will soon, perhaps tomorrow, as René and I are driving in to New Orleans to visit his mother. But I am afraid her accident may postpone our trip. Maybe not, though!

This is not a very good letter, but I will write again soon. Please give our affectionate regards to all your family, *y para ti, Arlette, recibe muchos abrazos y besitos de*

Emily

P.S. [From René]

My dear Arlette— My French is terrible, but perhaps you can teach me when I see you! My best regards to all the family.

René

* * * * *

[From Emily to Georges Delattre, Sr.]

Bay St. Louis, Miss.
New Year's Day, 1947

My dear M. Delattre,

I hope that our cablegram to you arrived a week ago announcing the arrival of the marvelous portraits and the beautiful view of the Seine! I cannot express to you the profound gratitude of the entire family for your magnificent gifts [. . .]. *When you see us in person, you will see that the portraits resemble us so perfectly that one would say that we are on the point of speaking. It is astonishing!* [. . .] [Emily's letter continues at length in like vein, and she adds, "*It must be wonderful to have a great talent like yours. We are so proud to be in possession of three of your paintings.*"]

We passed Christmas Day at home this year, and we were happy that Mrs. de M. was better and could walk into the dining-room that day on her crutches and eat Christmas dinner with us at the table. She has improved greatly and asks me to thank Arlette and all of you for your solicitude and your interest in her.

We had a pretty Christmas tree in our living-room this year, decorated with colored electric lights and imitation silver icicles. (Do you have this custom in France also?) For a week before Christmas we had placed all of our presents around the tree, and we opened them after twelve o'clock on Christmas Eve night. All of us received very lovely gifts from our relatives and friends, but the three paintings from you were by far the best gifts of all [. . .].

[Emily compliments Arlette's new dress and inquires if the de Montluzins' Christmas parcel, like the Delattres' reciprocal one, is still awaiting delivery.]

We appreciate very much, M. Delattre, your great kindness in offering to paint portraits of Mr. and Mrs. de Montluzin also, and we will send a photograph of Mr. de M. soon. Mrs. de M. does not have a photograph of herself which she likes, but she will have one made when she can. We hesitate, however, to accept so much of your time and trouble [. . .].

All our family send greetings to all of you, and our best wishes for 1947. And to you, again, we express our deepest gratitude.

Sincerely,
Emily de Montluzin

* * * * *

Bay St. Louis
February 23, 1947

Ma chère Arlette,

    Today, just when I was about to write to you, your letter written ten days ago arrived. We were all so happy to receive news from you, and I hope you will forgive me for my very long delay in answering your last letter—the letter with all the good news about Maurice and about your Riviera plans.[24]

    There is so much to say that I don't know where to begin. I believe, perhaps, that I should begin with Maurice, for what is more important than choosing a bride and starting forth on a happy married life? We are delighted to hear the news and would like very much to have a snapshot of his fiancée. Will you offer Maurice our congratulations, Arlette, and tell him too that we think his fiancée is a very lucky young lady! I hope that by this time they have been able to find an apartment. In every city in America the lodging situation is terrible, too. (Incidentally, Arlette, would you be kind enough to suggest to us something that they might like to receive from America as a wedding-gift? We would like to send them something that may still be hard to find in France. We would appreciate a suggestion from you and Mrs. Delattre.) But I could write on and on about such a happy event, and I must stop long enough to say how wonderful we think it will be for you to live at Cannes. I imagine life there must be like one long vacation! Since I have lived in Bay St. Louis for several years, I have learned to love the sight of the water so much that I do not believe I could be happy if I ever had to live inland. I suppose it will be the same with you if you go to live at Cannes. To me, life on a seacoast is the best life of all! I wish I thought we might visit you this summer, but I am afraid it will be impossible, Arlette. Mrs. de Montluzin is not able to walk yet, though her doctor is well pleased with her progress and says that now she will be safe enough to go riding in an automobile. She feels well, but it will be another month before she can begin to walk. She asked me to thank you for your good wishes and your thoughts of her.

---

[24] Arlette had told Emily that she was planning to leave home to live and open a shop in Cannes.

As for our visit to you, I dream of it all the time, and I am determined that sooner or later we shall come! During the war I bought a book called *Beyond the Riviera*, which described so charmingly the beautiful land of Provence, still lost in the shadows of the Middle Ages in its language, its legends, its customs, and its medieval ruins. I should love to travel through it, and especially to visit Grasse and see the fields of lavender, jasmine, and roses my book pictured so vividly! [. . .]

[Emily thanks Arlette for the Christmas gifts her family had managed to send despite France's postwar shortages and straitened economy—bottles of perfume for Emily and Venie, a "handsome scarf" for René, and "exquisitely embroidered handkerchiefs" for his father.]

I told you I would explain why I could not write to you ten days ago when the gifts arrived. Well, on February 14th Bay St. Louis had its big annual Carnival Ball, held each year during the Mardi Gras season. There are always a king, a queen, and a court to rule over the ball, and the identity of the king and queen is kept a secret until the very night of the ball. They are selected by a secret committee a month ahead of time, and everyone in town tries to guess who will be king and who will be queen, every year. This time René was asked to be the king and one of our friends was the queen! (It is customary never to have husband and wife as king and queen, so that even the two who are chosen do not know each other until the final night.) Of course, we had many preparations to make, since René entertained all the court and many other friends at a midnight supper and dance at a hotel after the ball. (The invitations to the supper dance said "His Majesty, the King, requests your presence at Hotel Reed at midnight, February fourteenth," and no one knew until that night who had invited them.) My mother and Harry arrived that morning from Dallas, and all of René's family attended the ball too <u>except his mother and father</u>! Isn't it a pity that they could not come? The theme of the decorations for the ball was "South America," and all the thirty [ladies of the] couples in the court wore bright-colored evening gowns. All the men were in costume. Only René was in full evening dress. I think he made a very gracious king-for-a-night (though perhaps my opinion does not count for much!). A photographer took many pictures, among them one of

René and me together. We ordered an extra copy to send you and will mail it to you as soon as it comes. We had a wonderful time that night. There were about 200 people at the hotel supper after the ball, and we danced there until 4:30. Then 17 of us went home with a friend of ours for breakfast, and we reached our own home at 6:30 in the morning! Mother and Harry were with us to the end and enjoyed every minute. They were here a week, and since the Mardi Gras season is so gay, we went to six parties during their visit! We spent Mardi Gras day itself in New Orleans, just as we did last year, and took some colored movies of the parades and the fantastic floats. I am enclosing a little paper (from under my Martini) from a French restaurant in New Orleans where we had dinner yesterday. You would probably feel at home in New Orleans, for one sees French on all sides there [. . .].

Please tell Mme Delattre that we are so happy to send more coffee and chocolate at once. Now that Mardi Gras is over, I had planned to prepare two boxes this week, and I am very glad you told me what you would like best to have. I shall try to get coffee in cans so that it will keep fresh. We are so sorry the carton of cigarettes was stolen, because that was the biggest part of M. Delattre's Christmas gift! We shall try again to send him some, and we hope for better luck.

I am to be in the next Little Theater play, *Angel Street* (or *Gaslight,* the movie version, with Charles Boyer and Ingrid Bergman. I have Ingrid Bergman's role, believe it or not!). We are to begin rehearsals tomorrow night and present the play in March. It was to have been given in December, but we postponed it.

I like the idea of your shop very much, Arlette. It should be a lot of fun! I shall try to help you think of a good name for it.

There is so much more I want to say about books and movies, but I must stop this time [. . .]. Write me soon again, *et recevez mes meilleurs baisers!*

All my love,
Emily

P.S. Hope you liked *The Lost Weekend.* I did, very much.

P.S. (Later) We have just returned from the movies, where the newsreel showed pictures of Grace Moore[25] during her last concert. We are grieved over her death, too, and we agree with you about the dangers of air travel recently.

* * * * *

Dallas, Texas
June 12, 1947

My dear Arlette,

Once again, a year later, I find myself in Dallas writing a letter to you without the aid of my dictionary! For that reason I'm sure that the majority of this letter will be in English [. . .].

[Emily writes at length about the numerous activities crowding her time, especially since she is now helping René at the drugstore. *"Every day is so full that I wish that each one had more than 24 hours! I believe that there are more things to do when one lives in a small town like Bay St. Louis, where one knows everybody and becomes 'involved' in all the doings of church, school, society, etc."*]

We were thinking of Maurice and his bride on the 24th and wishing them much happiness, and we could also picture all of the excitement of the wedding and of the two receptions following it. I know the luncheon at your home must have been delicious. I wish we had known your plans in time so that we might have helped your mother by sending some extra flour, sugar, etc., for the baking. It must, indeed, be hard to plan a party for fifty people when there are such severe restrictions on all food items [. . .]. [Emily wishes the bride and groom happiness and plans to send them a wedding present now that they are back from their honeymoon in Normandy.]

All of us are delighted with your description of your "petite maison americaine"![26] I especially like a very large living-room, and I prefer living in a

---

[25] Grace Moore (1898-1947), operatic soprano and film actress, killed in a plane crash in Denmark on January 26, 1947

[26] In Cannes, where Arlette had moved to open a shop

house which is all on one floor. You will find housekeeping much easier, I believe. It all sounds beautiful, Arlette. I am enclosing some pictures of the arrangement of modern American kitchens, as you asked me to, and before you become too amazed at such kitchen-magic, let me tell you that for most of us, too, kitchens like these are wonderful daydreams! The newly built homes have some of these wonderful things in them, and gradually many people are beginning to own one or two of them, but to a large extent they are postwar marvels that up to this date have not been produced in large enough quantity so that every home has all of them. In another year or two, however, they will be much easier to buy than they are now. Incidentally, we hope to start our own home this fall, and we shall plan our kitchen to accommodate all these wonders, so that, as we can purchase them, there will be a space already planned to receive them. Practically everyone nowadays has an electric refrigerator, except very poor families, or families who began housekeeping during the war when such things were no longer being manufactured. But the new refrigerators have large storage compartments where meats and vegetables may be quickly frozen and kept for weeks and weeks in perfect condition, ready for use whenever desired. The new electric stoves have time-controls that may be set so that food placed in the oven or on top will begin to cook at a certain time and stop cooking at a certain time! Thus you may put your dinner in the stove, set the dials for the time you think it will require to cook, and go out of your house knowing that the stove will automatically cut itself off at the proper time! The ovens have glass doors, too, so that you can see how things look inside without having to open the door. With the new sinks, you will never have to wash dishes! The dishes are stacked in an automatic dishwasher that swishes hot, soapy water over them, rinses them, and dries them with hot dry air in two minutes' time. Perhaps the most wonderful thing of all is the new Bendix washing-machine. You put the clothes in, sprinkle soap-flakes or granulated soap over them, press a button, and go wherever you want to go. The machine washes the clothes, rinses them several times, tosses them about in dry air until they are just right for ironing, and then cuts itself off![27] You never even have to hang

---

[27] Emily had as yet seen clothes washers and driers only in magazine advertisements and did not

them outside on a line! If all this is making you envious, just remember that I am as envious as you are. Some day I hope to own all these things, for every year it is becoming more of a reality and less of a dream. Every magazine is full of these pictures, and every store-window shows models of them. If you put your name on a waiting-list and wait for a few months, you can get one of these things even now. Needless to say, they are quite expensive, but all the time they are becoming less so. As for planning your kitchen, we find that the most practical way is to place your kitchen furnishings in a U-shape. That is, have your stove on one side of the room, your sink for washing dishes at one end of the room, and your refrigerator on the other side, across from the stove. Some of the pictures I'm sending will illustrate what I mean. This arrangement saves many steps and much time. We like to use a great many cabinets and drawers, too, instead of a closet or pantry. In this way all supplies are right at hand and yet out of sight. Most kitchens now provide a small space at one side for a table and chairs for informal meals, like breakfast or in-between-meal "snacks." I know that you can't get these electrical wonders right away in France, but neither can we here in America, right now. However, I think it's fun to look at them and plan to own them some fine day, don't you?

    You asked me, Arlette, about how much a trip from New York to New Orleans would cost. I inquired last week and found that if you should come in a Pullman (a sleeping-coach, you know) as I imagine you would want to do, the trip would cost about sixty dollars [. . .]. [Arlette should not even consider trying to find work to support herself during her hoped-for visit to America, Emily insists.] If you should ever come, we should want you to stay with us, and we should try to make your trip as much fun as we possibly could! It would be wonderful to know you, Arlette! I wish we could know all of you, either by your family's coming here or by our coming there. Sometimes I become very discouraged, too, about our proposed trip to France. And yet I feel sure that one of these days we shall know each other, don't you?

---

realize that they were two separate appliances.

I'm so glad you liked the picture taken of René and of me at the Carnival Ball. We went to a dance last month on top of the roof of a big hotel in Biloxi (about 40 miles away), and I wore the same dress. I think the dress you wore to the Bal de l'Opéra must have been perfectly exquisite. I believe M. Delattre was right—to me, nothing is lovelier than a white ball-dress, and the roses must have been the perfect touch. Your mother's dress was beautiful, too, I know. Imagine going to a ball with 9,000 people there! We all enjoyed looking at the clipping of the Opéra, especially Mr. de Montluzin. He remembers it well.

I have seen *Mrs. Miniver* and *All This and Heaven Too*, and I loved both of them. We saw Teresa Wright (who was killed, you remember, in *Mrs. Miniver*) in a new picture last week, *The Best Years of Our Lives*. It was very, very good. We also saw Frederic March in *Les Misérables* and enjoyed it for the second time, though so much of the wonderful novel is omitted that it is a shame. I'm glad you saw *Gaslight*. It was a coincidence that I should be playing in *Angel Street* about the same time, wasn't it? But I must stop, since I have so many clippings to include. Please give our love to all your family. We were glad the packages arrived safely. Write me soon again, please, Arlette! I love your letters!

With love,
Emily

* * * * *

Bay St. Louis
October 11, 1947

Dearest Arlette,

I'm afraid that my letter, like yours, will be in my own language this time, because I have much to say and only a short time this afternoon for writing. I do want to mail this letter to you today, however, even if it is a short one, because I want to ask you a question and to receive a reply from you as soon as possible. Then I shall write a really long letter like your charming ones.

But first, let me say how glad we all were to hear from you last week and to know that you are all well and enjoying making plans for your new home.[28] It is good news too about the baby-to-be! I know Maurice and Huguette,[29] as well as all of you, must be very happy. The wedding celebrations sounded wonderful– – The newlyweds surely received a good start for their married life, and perhaps all the happiness that day will be a good omen for their future. Please give them our best regards.

Did you read much in France about the terrible tropical hurricane which struck our beautiful Gulf Coast on the 19th of September?[30] You cannot imagine the destruction it left behind! I imagine bombed towns must look much the same as Bay St. Louis and Waveland[31] look now. The wind itself did much damage, but the chief terror was a huge tidal wave that suddenly appeared out of nowhere and rolled over the seawall all along the coast, sweeping away most of the buildings in its path, destroying all bridges, railroads, piers, and even paved streets along the water's edge. I am enclosing a few pictures taken afterwards which will give you some idea of how desolate our once-lovely Gulf Coast looks. The same scenes exist for at least 300 miles. Most of the loveliest homes and boulevards which we had were built along the beaches, and most of them were either destroyed completely or badly damaged. It will take years to repair and rebuild the roads alone. Many people, especially old people who could not swim, were trapped by the sudden rush of water and were drowned amid the wreckage of their homes. As for us, by some miracle our house and our drugstore remained standing, and none of us was hurt at all. At the drugstore there was some damage—the store is built on the beach, and the tidal wave tore away the back porch and the bathroom and swept away most of the foundation from

---

[28] The Delattre family was preparing to move from Le Perreux to the Avenue des Mérisiers in the neighboring suburb of Nogent-sur-Marne in the eastern outskirts of Paris.

[29] Huguette Panassié, Maurice Delattre's bride

[30] The 1947 hurricane predated the modern custom of giving names to hurricanes and tropical storms.

[31] Waveland, MS, the coastal town immediately to the west of Bay St. Louis

underneath.[32] But many other stores in the same block were completely demolished; so we feel very fortunate. Our house happens to be on a high point of land, so the water did not come nearer to us than the middle of the street. Many of our friends, however, lost everything they owned and barely escaped alive. We had no water, no electricity, no gas, no telephones for days and were not able to send messages out of town because all the roads and bridges were destroyed. My mother and brother in Texas were so frightened for our safety that they came by plane as far as they could, then took a train, then a taxi, and finally a boat to arrive in Bay St. Louis and find out for themselves whether we were still alive! They had heard on the radio that we were without food, water, etc., so they arrived laden with canned foods and fruit juices for us. It was all a terrible experience, but we can thank the good God that we came through it safely. René's drugstore was the only one left on the beach, and since the hospitals were full of injured people, he did a great deal of service. He used a military radio short-wave station to send word to New Orleans drug supply companies about drugs needed here, and the Coast Guard flew them here by helicopter for him!

Well, that is enough about the disaster here. Now for some much better news: René and I, too, are expecting a baby! We are very happy, of course! I think it should arrive about the middle of March, though my doctor in New Orleans says it might come in February.

As for the question: We had two packages wrapped and ready to send you on the day of the hurricane, but they were in the back of the drugstore and were soaking wet. We want to send two others so that they will arrive before Christmas, and what I want you to tell me is whether I should use your present

---

[32] Acting upon the advice of a local contractor, René de Montluzin and his father had recently replaced most of the drugstore's old heavy wooden pilings, sunk directly into the sandy beachfront embankment and presumed to be rotten, with new ones mounted on moisture-proof concrete bases. The hurricane demolished the nearby railroad bridge and swept its massive pilings like battering rams against all the waterside stores in the Bay St. Louis business district. Every building collapsed except for the de Montluzin drugstore, which lost its new supports (knocked off their bases by the railroad wreckage) and rested safely on its central row of old pilings the contractor had not bothered to remove.

address or your new one. Let me know as soon as you can! I must stop for now. Please give our love to all your family, and write soon!

Much love,
Emily

P.S. During the hurricane, we moved our beautiful portraits to a place of safety, just in case they might be harmed. You should see them in the frames we selected! We chose rather wide, pale gold, recessed frames. When you come, we shall see how you like them. I wonder which of us will win the contest.[33] I hope it will be you! We should love to have you come!

*   *   *   *   *

Bay St. Louis
November 10, 1947

My dear Arlette,

The news that you are really making your plans to travel to the United States next spring gives us the greatest possible pleasure! I wish you could see how happy we are! Already we're making a lot of beautiful plans, and our friends are also anticipating the pleasure of receiving and entertaining you. You ask what time would suit us best. We all think that perhaps it will be best if you arrive in the month of May or June. The baby is expected about the 18th of March, and by May I hope that I will be in good health again; besides, beginning in May the weather is always delightful here, and we will be able to do many things outdoors which would be impossible during the rains of April. We have read the information from the U.S. Embassy and will be happy to furnish you the necessary items. I will try to obtain the certificates within a week or two and will send them at once. In English, it will be wonderful to have you visit us, Arlette, and we are all eagerly waiting for the day your train from New York rolls into our little railway station. I hope you will not be disappointed in Bay St. Louis, which may seem very dull by comparison with the famous vacation spots of fabulous France!

---

[33] The contest concerned whether Emily and René or Arlette would be the first to visit the other.

But I believe that you will find the Mississippi Gulf Coast interesting, and I know that you will enjoy our trips to New Orleans. I shall have to practice speaking French with Mr. de Montluzin before you come, because I'm sure your English is a thousand times better than my French; but even if neither of us could speak the language of the other, I know that when you arrive, you will need no words of ours to tell you how very, very welcome you will be in our home.

Thank you for your congratulations about the baby. We are indeed very happy! If it is a boy, he will be named René. A girl will be named Emily Lorraine, and we shall call her Lorraine. We both think Lorraine is a pretty name, and it has some significance, too, since the de Montluzin family came from the province of Lorraine. We are happy to think you and Mme Delattre would like to send the baby something from Paris. You are so thoughtful and kind to want to do this. Whatever you choose will be beautiful, I know, and already I am grateful for it.

Today we packed two boxes, which we shall mail tomorrow and which we hope will help you in preparing your Christmas dinner. Since we are not sure of the sizes of articles to wear, we decided to make our Christmas remembrances to all of you this year in the form of those foodstuffs which we hear are still almost unavailable in France. We hope that nothing will be taken out of the boxes before you receive them. And oh, Arlette, I do so hope we have not delayed too long, and that the boxes will arrive before Christmas Day!

Bay St. Louis is still clearing away the wreckage of the storm. It will be years, I suppose, before our little town looks as pretty again as it did a few months ago. You asked about the Little Theater. It sustained only a little damage to its roof, and we are having the final play of 1947 in the first week of December—a minstrel, in which all the actors sing or dance. As for our bridge club, it is still meeting every Tuesday afternoon. Next Tuesday I shall be the one to entertain.

The description of your new home sounds really lovely. I know all of you must be very proud of it and very happy to be settled in it before the holidays. I like the name of your avenue[34]—"Wild Cherry Tree Avenue" in English. I

---

[34] Avenue des Mérisiers

wonder when I shall see its beauty for myself! There's no doubt about it, Arlette, you will be the one to win our little bet!

René and I have just read *The Foxes of Harrow*, an historical novel based on life in early New Orleans. We thought it exceptionally good and were particularly interested in the fact that its author[35] is a Negro. He is surely an excellent storyteller. Last week we saw the movie made from the same book and starring Maureen O'Hara and Rex Harrison. It was good, too, but not as well done as the book. Hollywood had changed the plot a great deal, which was rather disappointing.

Our newspapers and magazines have published many pictures during the last week or two of scenes photographed during the Communist riot in Paris a couple of weeks ago. We are all interested in the news concerning de Gaulle[36] and would like to know what you and your family think of the political situation. In a way, Ramadier's middle-of-the-road regime[37] sounds good—or do you think so?

All of us are well, though Mrs. de M. is still using one crutch. She is to have another X-Ray this week in New Orleans to determine whether she can soon discard it. René and I are driving in to New Orleans day after tomorrow for my monthly checkup with the doctor, too. Everyone joins me in sending affectionate regards to all of you. We hope Huguette is feeling well. Write soon again.

Much love,
Emily

---

[35] Frank Garvin Yerby (1916-91), author of numerous novels set in the American South

[36] Charles de Gaulle had disapproved of the adoption of a parliamentary system instead of a presidential system by the Fourth Republic, and he and his Gaullist party, the Rassemblement pour la République (RPR), were in political opposition.

[37] Paul Ramadier, Socialist and first postwar premier of France, whose regime (January 22-November 23, 1947) was the first of the 21 ministries (not counting cabinet reshuffles) of the unstable Fourth Republic. His expulsion of the Communist members of his cabinet in May 1947 had ended the three-way coalition (*Tripartisme*) among the French Communist Party (PCF), the Socialists (SFIO—*Section Française de l'Internationale Ouvrière*), and the Christian Democrat Popular Republican Movement (MRP) that had existed since 1944. Ramadier's ministry would fall less than two weeks after Emily wrote her letter.

* * * * *

Bay St. Louis
January 9, 1948

Dearest Arlette,

 Although we were happy to receive your last letter, our hearts were made very sad over the terrible news you told us about Maurice's and Huguette's little baby. We know exactly how heartbreaking such a tragedy can be, and we hope that you will extend to Maurice and Huguette our deepest sympathy and understanding of their loss. Perhaps it will not be long before they can try again to begin their family, and the next time they will surely be successful. I have many friends who also lost their first babies—somehow, it seems to happen very often, for some reason. Yet afterwards they had no trouble at all. I hope Huguette is regaining her strength by now and will soon be well again.

 As for me, I am feeling remarkably well and am being as careful as possible to do everything my doctor advises. René and I drove in to New Orleans two days ago for my regular monthly visit at his office, and he found me in perfect health. The baby should arrive about the 18th of March—and by the time you reach here, we shall both be able to enjoy every minute of your visit!

 I can't tell you how much we are all looking forward to having you here. Every day we say "When Arlette comes . . ." and we plan things we think you would like to do. I wish this country were not so large, so that we could meet you in New York and spend a while there with you! But with a new baby, I'm afraid that will be impossible. We shall have a wonderful time anyway, "'way down South"! If you don't know how to play bridge, I shall teach you at once when you arrive, because I am sure that there will be bridge parties given for you while you are here. And there will be swimming and visits to New Orleans—and lessons in French for me!

 This will have to be a short letter since I am enclosing the documents you asked for. I hope they will meet all the requirements of the U.S. Embassy [. . .].

 We had a very happy holiday season. Mother and Harry flew here from Dallas and spent ten days with us, which was all we needed to make our family circle complete. The weather was warm and sunny, and children were playing outside with their Christmas toys without even wearing a sweater! In our yard there are narcissus blooming, and roses, morning-glories, and poinsettias. It is not at all like typical January weather, so we are enjoying it to the utmost. Yes, we had a lovely tree, but over here they are decorated about a week before Christmas and are always taken down before New Year's Day.

Thank you for the lovely Christmas card. Mr. de M. beamed with pride when he read your father's note referring to him as "*le futur grand-père*"! By the way, did I tell you he had his 82nd birthday last month? He is well, and Mrs. de M. is improving. Only last week she began to drive the car again, but she still has to use one crutch for walking.

Please give our love to all your family and hurry with your preparations for coming to America! Write soon.

Much love,
Emily

P.S. Your last letter, <u>all</u> in English, really impressed me! I'm afraid I am the lazy one now. And to think you read *The Razor's Edge* without using a dictionary! That's wonderful, Arlette. I could never do that with a French book.

* * * * *

[The letter from Arlette Delattre that follows is one of only seven written by her or by other members of her family during the 1940s that survived Hurricane Katrina in 2005. (Edit.)]

[From Arlette]

Nogent 10/3 48 [March 10, 1948]

Dearest Emily,

I don't know how to excuse myself for not having written to you sooner except to say that many things have happened since your last letter that always made me put off writing until the next day.

First, I must say that at this moment we are thinking constantly of you because the day so long awaited by you and yours is arriving. We hope that everything goes well and that Easter Day of this year will add a René or a Lorraine de Montluzin to Bay St. Louis. All the final preparations must have tired you, and you must be eager to resume a normal life. Will you stay at home or go to a clinic [for the birth]? *We are impatient to learn the happy news and would be delighted if René or Mrs. or Mr. de Montluzin would let us know as soon as possible. Let the French first name of Baby be cabled quickly to the land of its origin! How spoiled and well cared for it will be by Mrs. de Montluzin and your mother. I hope to have the happiness of seeing this future baby "when I come to Bay St. Louis."*

My dear Emily, my engagement has been broken for three weeks.[38] *My parents have made me see reason regarding the great difference in age, and, besides, my ex-fiancé was divorced and had with him his fourteen-year-old daughter. In order to make me forget this whole thing, Papa has proposed to me to take a trip to America, and I have been busy ever since with the necessary papers. They are ready and the next steamboats will depart at the end of March and the beginning of April. My papers being in order, I can go get my ticket tomorrow if I want to. This is why I have been slow in writing to you, I wanted to know the time period involved to ask you if I would not be in the way when you will be getting over such a great event. Be sure that I want absolutely to make myself useful in your home or at the drugstore and that I would be distressed if it were otherwise. I do not want to be any trouble for you during my visit, and if after your having the baby you need rest, I will be very happy to help Mrs. de Montluzin at the house or Mr. de Montluzin and René at the drugstore. And then especially, we will take care of Baby, I will help you knit for him or make his little clothes. I wish I were already with you. The crossing will last 9 days. I don't yet know on which ship, surely not on the* De Grasse *or the* New Amsterdam, *which cost 265 and 335 dollars! For the French that's impossible when the dollar is*

---

[38] The correspondence provides no additional details of the engagement, since Arlette's preceding letters are no longer extant.

valued here at 305 francs. For the trip by railway from New York, your advice would be needed. People are allowed to take 50 dollars out of the country, but how does one make use of travelers checks? Perhaps Mr. de Montluzin would know.

You understand now why all my thoughts are in Bay St. Louis, for here in this letter I am saying to you: I come to America. Tell me above all *if I can come* and *if I won't be any trouble*. That's wonderful, isn't it? What a marvelous trip. The only thing wrong with it is that I'm afraid that Papa and Mama and Jojo will find the time very long, but I will write to them very often!

Had I told you that your two packages arrived in good condition and that their contents were more appreciated than ever? I am going at last to be able to thank you in person for all your kindnesses. Did you receive our Christmas package? I would hate to think it was lost. It got at least to New York, for I have the receipt of its departure from Orly.

Maurice has been sick for a month. He had jaundice, but he's well now.

The weather is magnificent and we would like our new little house in the middle of the Bois [de Vincennes] even more if we didn't have to fear break-ins by thieves, a frequent occurrence in our area.

What a pity that Mama can't come with me, your country tempts her too. This evening we saw *The Best Years of Our Lives* and we imagine the houses of Bay St. Louis to be like those of this film. What beautiful staging!

How was Carnival in New Orleans this year?

My dear Emily, I leave you for the present. I can say that all the things that remain to tell you I am saving for Bay St. Louis!

We are thinking of you and wishing you courage, good health, and especially a magnificent baby.

While waiting for the good news and the answer about the trip, everyone here sends you, Mr. and Mrs. de Montluzin, and René great affection. I embrace you very tenderly.

Much love always,
Arlette

* * * * *

Bay St. Louis
March 30, 1948

My dearest Arlette,

 First of all, let me tell you that René and I now have a beautiful little daughter, Lorraine, who was born on March 12th in a New Orleans hospital and who weighs 8 pounds today! She is like a little rosebud, really, and all of us are so happy and so proud of her that it will make you happy too when you see our joy! I would like to write pages about her, but ever since she was born, my eyes have been very weak, and I must try to make this letter short—probably an impossibility, since there is so much to say.

 As for my own condition, I am feeling quite well again and am regaining my strength rapidly. I remained in the hospital for ten days, and then René brought the baby and me back to Bay St. Louis by ambulance.[39] My mother is here with us, and I still have a nurse who comes each morning to help for a few hours until I am strong again. By the time you arrive, I'm sure I will be feeling better than ever before.

 Now for the wonderful news you wrote—that you will be able to come to visit us after all! Naturally, we cannot help being glad you decided to break your engagement, Arlette, because we are selfish enough to want you to come to America regardless of your ex-fiancé's unhappiness at losing you! We are all eagerly looking forward to having you with us, and we shall do all we can to make your visit a pleasant one. I am afraid you will be disappointed in Bay St. Louis, however, for it is a small, old-fashioned town and most of the homes are not as fine as the one you mentioned in *The Best Years of Our Lives*. But we shall try to help you have a good time, and we can hardly wait for you to arrive! It seems too good to be true that you are really coming!

---

[39] There were no complications with the birth. A long hospital stay and transport by ambulance for so long a distance were standard practice in 1948.

As to the information you wanted, I shall try to answer each question briefly:

(1) If you arrive during the first week of May, as your letter of March 25 says you plan to do, it will be a most convenient time for all of us. Be sure to get your ticket on the *Queen Mary* immediately. What a wonderful ship to have passage on! I envy you such an experience.

(2) We advise you not to take an "autocar" (or "bus," as we call them in America). They are very uncomfortable and one has no privacy. You should make the trip from New York by train. Be sure to get a Pullman ticket on the train named *The Crescent Limited*, because that train stops in Bay St. Louis. The other trains from New York will take you through here and on to New Orleans, so that you would have to come back from there hours later. The trip requires either 2 nights and one day, or vice versa, depending on what time you leave New York. When René and I were in Connecticut during the war, we would leave New York to come home on the *Crescent Limited* at about 1:30 P.M., reaching here about 8:30 P.M. on the day following. It is really a pleasant way to travel.

(3) I telephoned to inquire about the price of your train ticket, since I do not believe that will be included in your transportation from France. The ticket from New York to Bay St. Louis by Pullman (sleeping-cars, you know) will cost $64.63, and you will have to pay for your meals in the dining car too. Since you are allowed to bring only $50.00 with you, we shall arrange to have some additional money waiting for you in New York. Please, Arlette, don't feel badly about this arrangement—it is something you cannot avoid, and we are very happy to be able to do this small thing for you.

(4) I telephoned the office of the French consul in New Orleans to ask how we should have the money ready for you in New York, and he advised a very complicated procedure which would be confusing to anyone newly arrived in a foreign city, I think. So I plan to write tomorrow to a cousin of René's in New York, a Miss Alice Whitney, whose mother is Mr. de Montluzin's niece, and I shall ask her if it would be possible for her to meet you when you arrive on the *Queen Mary* and to help you secure your train ticket and find the right train. I believe she will be able to do this, and I know she will be glad to if she can. This

arrangement will be much easier for you, and I know it will make M. and Mme Delattre feel safer about you. As soon as I have her reply, I shall write you immediately, so that you will have definite information before April 30th.

(5) I think the New Orleans stores would be able to sell the beautiful clothing you described with no trouble at all. Our newspapers are full of advertisements of dresses, hats, and shoes at similar prices and more, and of course they are not French nor handmade. It would be easy to secure orders, I am sure. I think you are very enterprising to think of such a business venture! And I'm certain it will be successful.[40]

Now I have some bad news to tell you. Mrs. de Montluzin was operated on again today in New Orleans. Her broken hipbone has never healed properly, and it was necessary to operate once more and put in a silver plate to replace part of the injured bone. She is feeling all right by this time (the operation was 6 hours ago), and we believe this method will be successful. She will remain in the hospital for a week and will be on crutches for about four months, but the doctor assures us she will then walk again. She is very brave and patient, and she asked me before she left home to tell you she is looking forward to your visit very eagerly and can hardly wait for you to come [. . .].

I hope I have not forgotten to answer any of your questions. I have stopped to attend to my sweet, precious little Lorraine several times since I started this letter, and I'm afraid I have left out something I meant to say. The main thing is, however, that we are so happy you are coming, and that I shall write again about Alice Whitney before you sail. Don't let the rumors of war stop you![41]

---

[40] For the aftermath of this innocent paragraph see Emily's follow-up letter of March 30, 1948, and Arlette's reply of April 16, 1948.

[41] Tensions between the Western Powers and the Soviet Union had escalated in Europe in 1947 and early 1948, especially in Occupied Germany, where the Soviet Union was refusing to cooperate in plans to reunify the German economy and administration. Several weeks before Emily wrote her letter, Communists had taken over the government of Czechoslovakia by force, and the death of the Czech foreign minister, Jan Masaryk, had raised suspicions in the West. Fears of a new world war were widespread and would only intensify with the commencement of the Berlin Blockade by the Soviets in mid-June 1948. The American and British response—the Berlin Airlift—would begin on June 26, 1948, with American and British relief flights supplying all of Berlin's necessities until the blockade was lifted nearly a year later.

Grand-père René, *Père* René, my mother, and I would like to send our affectionate regards to all your family. I know that they will miss you terribly, but assure them that we will take good care of you and will try to supply their love while you are away from them! Write me again before you leave, to confirm your plans and dates.

Much love always,
Emily

* * * * *

[Arlette's enterprising plans to bring to America samples or photographs of handmade clothing, particularly specialty doll's clothing exhibited on expensive life-sized porcelain dolls, were already well underway. She had entered into advance discussions with Paris shops, and her intent was to initiate contacts with stores in New Orleans leading to transatlantic sales of the goods, with commissions for herself. Such plans aroused immediate and well-justified trepidations on the part of René, Sr., a cautious businessman who could foresee potentially serious legal problems looming ahead. He balked at expressing his views to Arlette himself, preferring to delegate to Emily, the family scribe, the unpleasant task of telling Arlette that she must not follow through with her plan to initiate purchase contacts with New Orleans stores. Emily's letter of April 1, 1948, designed to soften the blow with diplomacy and affection while putting a definitive end to the project, follows. Arlette's business acumen is self-evident in her reply of April 16, 1948, as well as the single-minded determination with which she, at the age of nineteen and in the teeth of the resistance of her host, René, Sr., insisted on persevering with her plan for marketing her line of expensive clothing for dolls. She would try again in New York before her return voyage to interest stores there in her scheme and would secure one tentative commission from Saks. The deal unfortunately would collapse because of the prohibitive price of the specialty dolls. Her total profits (from sales of dolls to several acquaintances in America) would be so disappointing that she would eventually give up the endeavor and turn her fertile business brain to a millinery enterprise instead. (Edit.)]

Bay St. Louis
April 1, 1948

Dearest Arlette,

Mr. de Montluzin has asked me to write you again today to tell you something about your plans which is causing him some anxiety. He has been thinking about your intention of bringing with you models and samples from some of the Paris shops. He feels that this would be very unwise and would involve you in endless complications, not only with our <u>customs</u> officials but also with our <u>income tax laws</u> if you were to sell any orders while in America. He says he wants you to come to visit us with no responsibilities, so that you will have a carefree, good time while you are here; and he is sure that if you engaged in any <u>business</u> enterprise while on a <u>visitor's visa</u>, you would soon be involved in many difficulties. I am writing to convey his wishes to you. I hope that this will not greatly disappoint you or cause you any embarrassment with the shops you have been asked to represent. We are all impatient to see you, and we want you to enjoy every minute of your visit with us [. . .].

[Emily's brief letter continues with details concerning the plan to arrange for René, Sr.,'s niece, Alice Doll, to meet the *Queen Mary* and assist Arlette upon her arrival, plus progress reports on Venie's hip surgery and on Lorraine.]

Everyone sends affectionate regards to you and your family. We can hardly wait to see you get off the train in Bay St. Louis!

Much love, always,
Emily

* * * * *

Bay St. Louis
April 7, 1948

Dearest Arlette,

I've just received a reply to my letter to Mrs. Doll in New York, and I am hurrying to let you know what she said. She is planning on meeting you at the boat if possible, and will wear a small, red-flowered hat, a black coat, and a black-and-white scarf. If the passengers' luggage is placed on the docks alphabetically, she will be standing near the "D" section. She is a small, gray-haired lady about sixty years old, and she used to speak French well, though she hasn't tried to for years. With your excellent knowledge of English, however, that doesn't matter at all!

In case something happens to prevent her coming to the docks, she suggests that you telephone her that you had landed and take a taxicab to her apartment. Be sure to take a <u>Yellow</u> Cab—they are very reliable and safe. Mrs. Doll's address is as follows [. . .]. [Emily provides the address and telephone number.]

The only thing that might prevent her meeting you at the boat is that she had two bad falls on the ice this past winter and is not quite recovered from them yet. However, she feels sure she will be able to come to the docks, and she plans on helping you to get your train reservations and to take the right train. The large New York stations are very confusing to any stranger, and you will be glad, I am sure, to have a little assistance! As I told you before, we will send some additional money to Mrs. Doll to keep for you, and we all hope so much that you will not worry about this necessary arrangement. We can hardly wait to see you, Arlette!

Mrs. de Montluzin is coming home by ambulance tomorrow. She is recovering from the operation very well indeed.

The baby is sweet and happy, and she gained a whole pound last week. She now weights 9 pounds!

I must stop. This will probably be my last letter to you before you sail. We are all looking forward so much to the first week of May and are anxiously awaiting a letter from you telling us that you are ready to sail! When you are in

New York, if you can, send us a telegram telling us when to expect you in Bay St. Louis so that we can meet your train here.

Everyone sends love to all your family. I wish we were going to have an opportunity to meet all of them too.

'Til the first week of May!
Emily

April 8th [1948]

Oh, Arlette, before I could mail this letter today, the wonderful [long-overdue] Christmas package from all of you arrived, and I had to open the letter and add this note to tell you how delighted all of us are with the beautiful gifts! The books look enchanting, and we can hardly wait to read them from cover to cover. All of us will enjoy them, I know. Mrs. de M. arrived today too from the hospital, and the exquisite handkerchiefs were here to greet her; we never saw any like them before. The baby's little cap, bootees, and mittens are so sweet and dainty, and I know she will look beautiful in them. And as for my gift, really, words are lacking to express how beautiful I think it is! I hope to use it every winter as long as I live, for I'll take the best of care of it. Imagine my owning a bed jacket from a wonderful shop on the Champs-Élysées [. . .]. I used to study about the Champs-Élysées when I was in school and taking French lessons, and I never dreamed I'd own something from there myself—or that part of my baby's layette would come from there either.

I must stop—am in a hurry to give my daughter her dinner! All the family ask me to express our gratitude to all of you for your lovely gifts. They are surely worth waiting this long delay for!

Much love,
Emily

* * * * *

[From Arlette]

Nogent, 16/4 48 [April 16, 1948]

My dear Emily,

I had just written you a long, 9-page letter when your second and then third letters arrived, so I'll begin again.

What joy when the news of the birth of your little Lorraine arrived! We send you our sincere congratulations and our wishes for good health for you and Bébé. Your whole family must be thrilled over this happy event, and Lorraine must be the center of everybody's admiration. I am in a hurry to see her, we speak of her so often. Already 9 pounds, it's marvelous! What a pity that Mrs. de Montluzin had to undergo another operation. I hope that this one will have a better result than the other and that she can now enjoy good times with you and her granddaughter. To her as well we send all our wishes for health and a prompt recovery. She is very courageous to have borne up under so much suffering since her distressing accident.

Thank you very much for all the information I had asked you for concerning my trip and for all the numerous details. And in response to all the trouble you have gone to for me, I am truly sorry to have been the cause of so much inconvenience in your family. Don't worry, my ticket is reserved on the Queen Mary *for the 30th of April, Cabin 865 B Deck, but one can only know 8 days before the departure the exact day and time of arrival in New York. The crossing takes 5 days. I expect to arrive on Tuesday, May 4. You were very kind to have thought of asking Mrs. Doll to come get me. That relieves my parents, for one must feel terribly alone in a big city like New York.* [But] *I received at the same time as your 3rd letter a letter from a childhood friend who lives in South Nyack near New York, whom I had asked when I thought I would be alone in N.Y. to come get me at the boat. Meanwhile you have told me that Mrs. Doll would come also. I know that waiting among the crowd at the dock is very fatiguing and sometimes lasts 3 or 4 hours. Mrs. Doll, who is not yet fully recovered from her falls, as you tell me, would certainly be worn out. I would like to avoid that for her and to go see her at her apartment. I would like that very much. My friend Jacqueline Fiola will wait for me at Pier D, will recognize me at once, and will* guide me to the "Yellow Cab" that you advise me to take to Mrs. Doll, whom I shall let know ahead of time. Don't you think that this arrangement will avoid Mrs. Doll's staying long hours standing? I am going to write her to thank her and I will tell her my arrival date [. . .].

As for the arrangement you propose about money, I hesitate to accept, for I will have done all I can to stay within my allotted $50, since my voyage, going and returning, is paid for. I will economize as much as possible, because it is troubling, you must understand, to be already in debt to Mr. de Montluzin even before arriving in Bay St. Louis. You four have been really too wonderfully attentive to me, and I am so sorry to have involved you in such complications. I have noted down the train you advise me to take and the Cook Agency has reserved for me, but their information shows a price of $102 round trip in 1st class sleeping cars. I will see about the right price once I am in New York and get the ticket.

Reassure Mr. de Montluzin about the fears he had concerning the samples that I must bring with me. I am not bold enough to risk bringing with me any compromising merchandize which might get my visa revoked and get you into trouble. I have checked on all the information and precautions concerning what I will bring in. _I am in compliance_. And anyway, I'm only bringing with me photos and sketches of the collections, which I will declare at Customs, and 4 doll samples which I will declare as gifts and which will give Lorraine a lot of pleasure for several years. The rest, blouses and shoes, will go through Customs as my own personal things. Therefore, don't worry; I am prudent and don't like cheating. And my immense appreciation of all that I owe you will serve as my guide and I will not risk getting involved in any dangerous enterprises. My interest is only in establishing relations between the houses I have been dealing with in Paris and stores in New Orleans, so that I will not be living entirely at your expense during my visit. You may _be sure_ that I will comply with French and American regulations and that I will declare what is necessary at Customs. I have not planned to take any commissions in the United States but simply to initiate ties between French and American business houses. The Paris houses will reserve a commission for me here in Paris. Thus, I repeat, don't be worried about any great commercial enterprise on my part; I don't want to cause you any trouble.

[Arlette chats about the baby, Emily's recovery from her delivery, etc.]

[. . .] *All my friends tell me, "You are lucky to be leaving for America!" Last Sunday we had them here at the house for a farewell get-together before the great departure, and I assure you the whole topic of conversation was Bay St. Louis. And we danced to the sound of phonograph records with New-Orleans-style music.*

These last weeks have been very full of shopping and preparations. Will I have time before April 30th to go at least once to the Eiffel Tower to take panoramic shots for you? Mama is dreading this April 30th and wishing already for the day of my return. There are moments when she advises me to stay with you for a long visit because a trip of this importance doesn't happen often in a lifetime; and other moments when she tells me to come back soon and especially not to get married in America! Leaving will be hard, all the more so because Mama and I are always together. I have promised to write to her every day. Really, everyone would like to leave to go see you, especially Jojo.

It seems to me that I still have a host of things to tell you, so many that I can't remember them all. I am so happy that I will get to know all of you at last as well as your marvelous America. I hope that Mrs. de Montluzin is recovering quickly and that your eyes are better as well.

As soon as I know the exact date of arrival, I'll write, and I'll send you a telegram from New York. Thank you again a thousand times for all you are doing for me. Again, I thank Mrs. Doll. And above all, be assured as to everything that's worrying you, I will be prudent.

We send our wishes for good health for you, Mrs. de Montluzin, and Bébé, as well as our best affection for Mr. de Montluzin and René, the happy papa. For Lorraine, give her a thousand big kisses for all of us. I am in a hurry to do that myself!

I embrace you with all my heart, Emily.
Arlette

P.S.   Ready to sail!

* * * * *

Excerpt from Arlette's diary, her *journal*,
which she kept during her visit to America;
text given exactly as written[42]

New York! Statue of Liberty! Manhattan! Green! Red! Stop! Go! Crowds! Crowds everywhere! Lights! Headlines! Is that the America I am dreaming of for years?

I get dizzy in my train. For years I was planning to visit my family in New Orleans, the De Montluzin's, I had pictured out of their letters, out of my imagination, that was nearly to become true.

Since Mobile, Alab. the Pullman goes slowly for we are passing over wooden bridges built on muddy and rough currented bayous.

Two days ago, in New York, I was wearing fur coat, and now I see a bushy blossoming along the railroad track. We are passing through Ocean Springs, Biloxi, Gulfport, and Pass Christian. I never saw such lovely and beautiful sceneries. That reminds me an old famous tell about New Orleans "She tells her beads and wears azaleas in her hair." Here it is— Azaleas all over, little wooden churches hidden among azaleas groves; those burst into joyous bloom for Mardi Gras. Oleanders flourish in March and magnolias in May. And when the trees are filled with flowers the mockingbird goes mad with glee. Whenever the train stops I can hear that black & white bird's melodis [*sic*].

The train is now rolling along a 3 miles bridge between Pass Christian & Bay St Louis; it was destroyed by fire and tempest several times in a century—the view of the Bay with its shore of secular oaks & pine-trees is pretty impressive.

Here am I getting off the train, the Red Cap is there helping me out, I am the only one to stop at Bay St Louis. Isn't it strange, ten days ago, I was in Paris,

---

[42] Arlette typed her journal after she returned to France, and she sent a complete copy (in English) to Emily and René de Montluzin. That copy was lost in Hurricane Katrina in 2005. Before her death in 2006 Arlette sent Emily a four-page handwritten excerpt of the portion of her journal describing her arrival in Bay St. Louis in 1948.

I am still wearing my French dress, I still think and sometimes even talk in French, nothing really makes me realize I have reached the end of a long trip.

Green and well-kept lawns, palmtrees and oleanders trim the small railroad station.

What happens, suddenly! The *Marseillaise* franeticly [sic] bursts into my ears! Here come from the platform end my cousins René Jr & his wife, making their greetings in their own way. Where are the words I had prepared for days especially for that meeting?

Though we meet for the 1st time, I have the wonderful feeling that we have always been knowing each other, the warmth of their welcome is sweet to me, I was afraid without really knowing it. Let me look at them, they really do look like their pictures.

René is now driving home. On the front porch stairs, my old cousin René De M. Sr is standing there waiting to welcome "in French" his young french cousin.

III

Interlude
Summer 1948

Arlette arrived at the Bay St. Louis railway station at 8:30 on an early May evening to be embraced joyously by René and me and driven across town to her home-away-from-home for the next three months, where Mr. and Mrs. de Montluzin eagerly awaited her with baby Lorraine and with her father's paintings on the wall to greet her as she entered.

Since she had been told not to expect a mansion, she must have been pleasantly surprised by the de Montluzin home atop a bluff facing the wide expanse of the bay and surrounded by a grassy lawn with oak, pecan, and fig trees and a magnolia in full bloom. Built in the plantation style of the late 1800's by Ludovic and Reine and finished in 1900, it was an elevated, two-story white frame house with a gallery across the entire front. Both the first and second floors were centered by a wide wainscoted hall with two spacious bedrooms and a bathroom on each side, for the family in 1900 was large and required eight bedrooms. The interior walls throughout were made of narrow white beaded boards, and the ceilings were fourteen feet high.

At the rear of the first floor hall was a rectangular dining-room, its exterior wall of windows lined by a shelf of ferns and facing the branches of two great fig trees. Adjoining it were a breakfast room and kitchen, each opening onto its own small porch and stairs.

At the time that Arlette arrived, the four bedrooms and two baths on the second floor were no longer needed, since Mr. de Montluzin was the last of Ludovic's and Reine's children to survive, and the upstairs area was now used for storage and for the personal effects and furniture left behind by his sister Corinne and two of his brothers, Alfred and Roger. The front windows allowed the breeze from the bay to sweep through the bedrooms, where the upper two feet of the walls separating them had been left open by design for this cooling purpose.

Arlette's bedroom (René's before our marriage) was by common consent the most desirable one in the house. It was just to the left of the entrance, and its floor-length French windows opened onto the gallery. From them in the mornings Arlette could see the sun rise over the bay, and in the evenings the moon was reflected in its water. Her bed was a tall mahogany antique crowned by a satin-lined tester, and her room included a Victorian marble-topped dresser, spacious armoire, caned chair, and her own wide lavatory on one wall.

Although Venie was still on crutches, everything that she, her young maid Ernestine Betts, and I could do to prepare for Arlette's visit had been done. Admittedly, the front porch needed a new coat of paint, but that project had been delayed because of the necessity for postwar economizing.

Arlette had brought several exquisite, handmade baby dresses and a lace-trimmed white organdy bonnet for Lorraine, whom she christened her *petite poupée rose*.[1] It was her own clothes that presented an immediate problem, all of them except for evening dresses being made of lightweight wool and hence unwearable in the hot summer weather on the Gulf Coast. We had already sent out invitations to a reception at the Hotel Reed to introduce our French cousin to our friends, and she had nothing to wear! It was Venie who came to the rescue. In a trunk upstairs she had many lengths of dress materials, bought on impulse now and then for future use. With some of them and with pictures from *Vogue* and *Simplicity* pattern books Arlette and I sought the help of a local seamstress,

---

[1] "Little pink doll"

who understood the emergency and skillfully made the summer dresses that were needed for everyday use and for the many social occasions to come.

Arlette's immediate daytime introduction to Bay St. Louis was a drive along Beach Boulevard, miles of winding coastal road on the western edge of the bay, past white sand beaches, green marsh grass, herons wading in the shallows, pelicans resting on pier pilings, and long stretches of seawall with waves slapping against the abutments and seagulls wheeling overhead. On the way I pointed out Our Lady of the Gulf Catholic Church, assuming that Arlette, being French, would wish to attend Mass. Matter-of-factly, she told me that I was under a false assumption. She was no longer Catholic, she announced. The war and the Nazi Occupation had put an end to the Catholic faith of many people in France, and she had become, she said, a Freethinker, believing in Nature. Clearly that was that. There would be no need for us to drop her off at Mass each Sunday on our way to our own service at Christ Episcopal Church.

The reception at Hotel Reed was a great success. All the guests wanted in their turn to entertain the beautiful French girl who loved the sun and strolled every day in her bikini (the first ever seen in Bay St. Louis) on the beach in front of our house. Morning coffee parties, dinner parties, and swimming parties in private pools were given for her. The young bachelors in town vied for the privilege of taking her out. René and I drove with her to New Orleans to show her the city and to introduce her to her other cousins there, and often we rode with her along the coast to Gulfport and Biloxi or, in the opposite direction, to Waveland and Clermont Harbor. One of her New Orleans cousins, Edgar de Montluzin, came for her in his car and drove her to Mobile to spend the day at Bellingrath Gardens, and several times René and I took her to the Broadwater Beach Hotel in Biloxi for dinner and dancing.

Her days were pleasantly filled with visits to see the new babies of some of my friends, as the postwar Baby Boom was by now in full swing. She and I took long walks in our neighborhood, pushing Lorraine's stroller ahead of us and teaching each other new words like "hydrangeas" in French and English. She picked ripe figs for breakfast and took a rocking chair from the porch out into the front yard so that she could sit in the sun as she knitted for Lorraine. She sent long letters to her family and every day wrote in her journal. In the Europe that she had left behind, the Berlin Blockade by the Soviets had begun and American and British relief planes were flying nonstop to airlift supplies to the beleaguered city, but all that was far from our minds that summer.

At the drugstore she had many conversations in French with René, Sr., to his great delight. It was there that she discovered Kleenex, another modern wonder unknown at that time in Europe. A businesswoman at heart, she conceived the idea that since her father's printing company had ample access to paper, he might introduce a similar product to European markets and make a fortune. Georges, Sr., however, scoffed at the ridiculous suggestion of handkerchiefs made of paper to be used once for blowing one's nose and then thrown away, and her very good suggestion came to naught.

One major event during her visit was Lorraine's christening at Christ Episcopal Church. The baby wore a long white dress which had been handmade by Venie for René to wear when he himself had been baptized, and of course she wore the lace-trimmed organdy bonnet Arlette had brought from Paris. She behaved with great decorum during the ceremony and afterwards at a lawn party at home for her godparents and other guests.

Soon after Arlette's arrival a permanent building was erected for the Little Theater, of which she had read so much in my letters. A vacant lot for it had been offered by a local doctor, and since an Army Air Force base in Gulfport was being dismantled, two of its surplus buildings were placed on a barge and floated to Bay St. Louis to form a T-shaped theater. It was painted barn-red in New-England style, and our French cousin enthusiastically climbed a ladder one day to help with the painting.

Arlette's admiration of the seafood that Venie set on the table almost every day was boundless. She had never before tasted crab gumbo or other Creole dishes. She reveled in Venie's oyster soup, oysters in patty shells, boiled shrimp, shrimp Creole, and crab meat served in many ways, not to mention flounder, redfish, and trout.

There was always an abundance of such seafood that cost the family nothing. A local fisherman had built himself a wharf between two buildings near the drugstore, and since he had no trust in banks, he brought his money to René, Sr., to keep for him and to dole out to him (always following stern questioning) whenever he wanted to spend some. His money was kept separately in a wooden cigar box in the office safe, along with the narcotics supplies and the business cash. To show his appreciation to his personal banker, he often appeared at the drugstore with fish, shrimp, live crabs, or a bushel of oysters. Sometimes, in fact, Venie would exclaim desperately, "Oh, Johnny! Not again!" On these occasions the boy who delivered prescriptions by bicycle to shut-in customers would be set to work on the back porch of the store to shuck the oysters and clean the fish before they were taken to the house. Arlette was charmed by the arrangement.

In spite of the fact that her English was exceptionally good, at times there were memorable *faux pas* and necessary explanations of slang and idioms. When René remarked one day that he had heard that Mr. Smith had kicked the bucket, Arlette, ever alert to a new expression, immediately asked, "What bucket?" At the breakfast table one morning after she had had a date the night before, she said very seriously, "Tell me, René, what is a cold potato? My date said to me when he left last night that I am a cold potato." René laughed and told her that perhaps her date had expected a goodnight kiss. "Oh, no!" she exclaimed. "Always I shake the hand!"

She was puzzled when on a drive along the beach on a windy day we exclaimed about the whitecaps on the water. "Where are caps?" said she. "I don't see any caps!" But the most memorable occasion occurred when she climbed out of the pool at a swimming party and, a shower in mind, started toward the house calling back over her shoulder "I'm going in now to take a douche." Every female guest's eyes swiveled instantly to me, and I gave Arlette a quick vocabulary lesson as soon as we were back in our car! In French, of course, she would have been perfectly correct.

We often laughed to discover how many words were the same in both our languages, though the pronunciations were very different. On a drive toward Waveland one day I pointed out to her the house built by the notorious pirate Jean Lafitte. She could not understand the word "pirate," and I tried to explain in terms like "a very bad man on a ship, who robs other ships and kills people."

Sudden comprehension! "Oh! A *pee-rot*!" she exclaimed. "Pirate" in English was "*pirate*" in French but with no similarity at all in the sound!

The end of her visit came all too soon, and she left René and me at the railway station promising her that we would see her again in France. In a letter she wrote on July 30 aboard the *Queen Mary* she said, "*Monsieur de Montluzin, I saw you waving your handkerchief when the train left, for as soon as Emily and René were out of sight on the platform, I ran to the window to see Bay St. Louis and the porch of your house from the bridge one last time. And you can imagine how moving it was to see you and not to be able to cry thank you once again.*"

Arlette's friend in Nyack as well as Alice Doll in New York took great care of her for several days, showing her Radio City Music Hall, Rockefeller Center, and Riverside Cathedral and going with her to shop at Macy's and Saks. Fortunately, her father, ignoring the French government's ban on taking more than $50 out of the country, had recently simply sent her the equivalent of $100 in a letter, and she used it carefully. She wrote, "At Macy's I bought some Pyrex bowls, two sheets, some other plastic things. At Saks, a waterproof jacket for Jojo and shirts for him at Crawford's, at McCreery's white rubber snowboots for Mama; at the Rockefeller Center I found a brown gabardine dress for me for only 12 $. I am glad, because I was very careful about the prices and made really good bargains. There is such a big choice in New York."

Several of her Nyack friends took her to the *Queen Mary* to be of help with her luggage. She had three valises, a box with all her recent purchases, and another box containing an electric MixMaster and several records of popular songs—goodbye gifts from one of her Bay St. Louis dates. Ship rules permitted only two visitors to accompany a passenger to a cabin; but she needed help with so much to carry, and, she wrote, "asking a very impressive officer, I could get a pass for three of them. So, they could visit the ship until 9:30. You see, I left the States with another more favor of the American people!"

The *Queen Mary* sailed at midnight, and Arlette stayed on deck until nearly two o'clock, watching the stars come out and America disappear.

Her letter says very simply, "*It is not every day that one leaves New York. . . .*"

2. (top) Emily de Montluzin in 1941 (photo used by Georges Delattre for her portrait)
3. (bottom) René de Montluzin, Jr., Chief Pharmacist Mate at the U. S. Coast Guard Academy in New London, CT (1944; photo used by Georges Delattre for his portrait)

4. (top) Emily in New London, CT, during World War II, wearing a wool suit she later sent to Arlette in one of the family's first packages (photo 1944)
5. (bottom) René in New London, CT, during World War II (1944). He inscribed this photo to Arlette's family, "My four years' service to my country was given voluntarily with the determined desire in my heart that one day the world would find itself at peace—and the honor and glory restored to France!"

6. (top) Corinne de Montluzin, aged 17 (1887)
7. (bottom) Georges Delattre, Sr. (1945)

8. (top) Camille Delattre, wife of Georges Delattre, Sr., with their son Maurice
9. (bottom) René Delattre, brother of Georges Delattre, Sr., in his French army uniform

10. (top) Arlette Delattre, aged 17 (1946)
11. (bottom) Georges Delattre, Jr. ("Jojo"), aged 13 (1945)

12. (top) Georges Delattre, Jr., and Arlette (1950)
13. (bottom): Georges Delattre, Sr., at his easel

14. (top) The de Montluzin family home built by Ludovic and Reine, 1899-1900, as Arlette first saw it in 1948 (photo taken in 1947)
15. (bottom) View of the Bay of St. Louis from the front porch of the de Montluzin family home (1949)

16. (top) Arlette's room in the de Montluzin family home as it looked in 1948
17. (bottom) René de Montluzin, Jr., in the hall; Georges Delattre's newly arrived portrait of René, Sr., visible behind him

18. (top) Arlette, photographed in the first bikini worn in Bay St. Louis (1948)
19. (bottom) Arlette, ready for a drive to visit Bellingrath Gardens in Mobile, AL (1948)

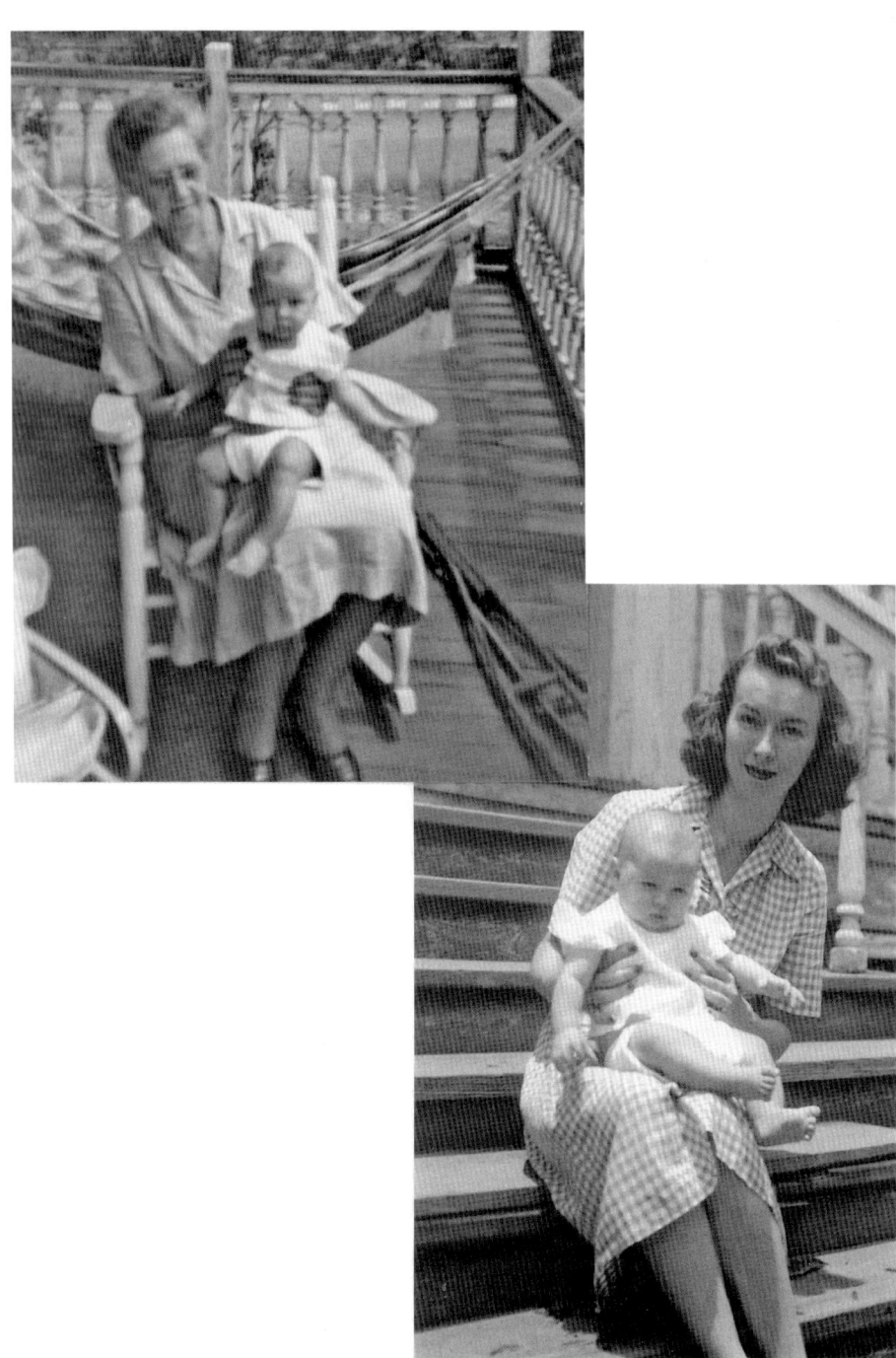

20. (top) Venie de Montluzin with Lorraine on the porch of the family home, her crutches beside her (1948)
21. (bottom) Emily de Montluzin with Lorraine on the front steps of the family home (1948)

22. (top) Left to right: Lorraine, René, Harry Hosmer (Emily's brother), and Venie de Montluzin (January 1949)
23. (bottom) Emily Gayden Hosmer (Emily's mother) with Lorraine (1950)

24. (top) Emily (seated) in Bay St. Louis Little Theater's production of *Angel Street* (1947)
25. (bottom) Emily (far left) in another scene in *Angel Street* (1947)

Bay St. Louis, Mississippi
April 29, 1949

Van Horn's
Philadelphia, Pa.

Gentlemen:

In accordance with the terms of your telegram of this date, I am enclosing a check for $4.00 as deposit on two costumes needed by our local Little Theater for the play "My Sister Eileen". The balance will be paid C.O.D.

The costumes will be used for three nights performance plus one dress rehearsal, May 18, 19, 20, and 21st.

Following are the two costumes and sizes:
(1) Russian doorman: 32-inch (length) trousers, 38-inch waist, 42 coat.
(2) Chewing-gum girl: 36 bust, 26 waist, 36 hips

Please send immediately to Mr. Roland Weston, Treasurer, Bay St. Louis Little Theater, Bay St. Louis, Mississippi.

Very truly yours,
Mrs. René de Monthigny
Production Chairman, Little Theater

26. Emily's letter to the Van Horn Company ordering costumes for the Bay St. Louis Little Theater's production of *My Sister Eileen* (1949)

27. (top) René de Montluzin, Jr., king of the Bay St. Louis Carnival Ball, with Emily, a maid in the ball (1947)
28. (bottom) Lorraine de Montluzin, a train-bearer to the queen of the Bay St. Louis Carnival Ball (1953)

29. (top) René, Sr., and Venie, with René, Jr., and Lorraine (Easter Sunday, 1953)
30. (bottom) Portrait of René de Montluzin, Sr., painted by Georges Delattre in 1948; destroyed by Hurricane Katrina

31. (top) Georges Delattre's landscape of a viaduct over the Marne at Nogent, painted in the early 1940s before its demolition by the retreating German army during World War II
32. (bottom) Jacques Baron and Arlette Delattre (New Year's Eve, 1953)

33. (top) Arlette with Maurice and Huguette's daughter Dorothée in Nogent-sur-Marne; behind them, one of Georges Delattre's paintings on his easel (1966)
34. (bottom) Jacques Baron and René at Fontainebleau (1966)

35. (top) The de Montluzin drugstore in Bay St. Louis, MS, rebuilt in 1897 after the 1878 building was destroyed by fire
36. (bottom) René with his father and a customer in the drugstore (1949)

37. (top) René filling a prescription with Lorraine watching (1955)
38. (bottom) The frosted glass partition separating the front of the drugstore from the prescription area; pharmaceutical antiques displayed on counter

39. (top) Lorraine and her uncle, Harry Hosmer, at the round table in the drugstore office, with pharmaceutical antiques displayed behind them (1967)
40. (bottom) The wreckage of the drugstore left behind by Hurricane Camille on August 17, 1969

41. (top) The de Montluzin family home, converted into the popular bed-and-breakfast Bay Town Inn, decorated for Christmas (2004)
42. (bottom) The wreckage of the de Montluzin family home after its destruction by Hurricane Katrina on August 29, 2005

43. (top) Living room in Emily's home in Bay St. Louis before Hurricane Katrina; on the left walls the Delattre portraits of Emily and René and the Delattre landscape of the Seine (photo taken 2003)
44. (bottom) Living room after Hurricane Katrina; seven-foot-high waterline visible (August 2005)

45. (top) Sun porch in Emily's house, filled with antiques from the old family home, before Hurricane Katrina (photo taken 2002)
46. (bottom) Sun porch as it looked after Katrina (photo taken September 2005)

47. (top) Wreckage in Emily's home after Hurricane Katrina (photo taken September 2005)
48. (bottom) Wreckage along the beach front at the head of de Montluzin Avenue in Bay St. Louis after Hurricane Katrina (photo taken November 2005)

IV

New Times, New Challenges
1948-1955

Bay St. Louis
July 12, 1948

Dearest Arlette,

Forgive me if my letter this time is almost entirely in English. I'm writing at night, and since I know I will soon be so tired and sleepy that I shall have to go to bed, I shall use English because it comes to me so much faster!

There is so much to say that I hardly know where to begin. First of all, let me say that your letters and cards made us very happy and yet very sad too, because we miss you terribly. I can hardly believe yet that you have come and gone—it seems like a dream! But we are so glad that you had such a wonderful time in Washington and in New York. Captain and Mrs. Goodwin were lovely to entertain you so royally, weren't they? I had their address, you know, so I wrote them a thank-you note myself [. . .].

[Emily compliments Arlette on her ability to make friends in a foreign country and gives her news of some of her Bay St. Louis acquaintances. As for Lorraine,] she is five months old today, and Mr. de M. gave her a beautiful highchair as a 5th-month birthday present! It comes from McDonald's and is the newest style—it can be disconnected in the center so that it forms a low chair and a low table, as well as being a traditional table-level highchair. I took some pictures of Lorraine today sitting in it, and I'll send them to you in my next letter. She weighs 17 lbs and 5 ounces today, and she tries her best to stand up already. Of course, I discourage that—she's much too young!

Now I shall try to tell you many little news items as I happen to remember them—

Mrs. de Montluzin's X-ray was very encouraging, showing much progress in healing. The doctor thinks that after one more X-ray next month, he will be able to tell her to throw away her crutches [. . .]. [Here follow many local news bulletins, among them the following:] I had a birthday this week, and René gave me two more of the silver tumblers like the ones he served mint juleps in the night before you left—remember? [. . .] Believe it or not, our house now has a new front porch and new steps! The carpenters have been here all week. They tore the old porch and steps away entirely and built it all again of new lumber. Next week we hope to have painters come to paint the house. I'm sorry it had not been done before you came! [. . .] We went to the Little Theater play [. . .] and enjoyed it very much. I'm enclosing a page from the program. Although your name is not spelled correctly, at least your help in painting the theater was appreciated! [. . .] Eve Joyce says that she's going to send you a pair of stockings—something new, nicer than nylon. Her husband's company makes them. (P.S. René just told me she brought the stockings today to the drugstore, and I'll send them with the next package.)

Please, Arlette, ask your mother and father to forgive me for never having written to them while you were here. You know that I intended to, but I keep so busy all day long with Lorraine. By the way, tonight I <u>tried</u> and <u>tried</u> to sing her to sleep with *America the Beautiful*, and when I couldn't, I tried *La Marseillaise*, and she went to sleep at once!

Write us soon again and tell us all you've been doing since you arrived home. I know your beautiful little house looked very good to you, and I can imagine how happy you and your family were to be together once again, with so much to talk about! René wants to add a note; so I'll stop here with a heart full of love to all of you from every one of us [. . .].

Emily

[From René]

Ah! Darling Arlette! Poor René, Jr.—he is very <u>sad</u>—no one to listen to his French any more—he has no one to tease—he misses his little sister Arlette! Hey, Jojo! Are you reading this letter over your sister's shoulder? I wish my French were as good as your English. How was your trip to England? We look forward to your letters, Arlette, and we are anxiously awaiting the arrival of your journal. The first chance I have, I will send you a portion of the story about my great-grandfather.[1] Em has just made some good highballs—wish you were here to drink one with us tonight. All my love to you and the family,

Your cousin René, Jr. [. . .]

* * * * *

Monday Morning
July 19, 1948

Good morning, my cousin!

It is 9:30 in the morning, and at this moment I believe that you are en route to New York after two days of sightseeing in Washington.[2] *Oh, Arlette, we have thought of you <u>all</u> <u>day</u> <u>every</u> <u>day</u> since you left, and really we have been lost without you. You have become one of this little family so completely that now the house seems big and empty, and I don't like to look at your room. We talk about you constantly, trying to imitate your cute accent, wondering what you must be doing, saying how much we miss you. Every day I say to Lorraine, "Bonjour,*

---

[1] Louis de Montluzin (1784-1850), a lieutenant in the Second Regiment of the Chasseurs à Cheval (lancers) in Napoleon's Grande Armée, whose wartime experience included service in Poland, Spain, Austria, Russia (where he was gravely wounded, receiving seven lance thrusts to the body), and the Waterloo campaign.

[2] This was a slight miscalculation in the timing of Arlette's return journey.

mon ange! Bonjour, ma poupée rose! Comme tu es belle ce matin! As-tu bien dormi?"[3] *and a lot of other things I've heard you say to her. I'll never forget the night of your departure, Arlette—how terrible it was to know that you would go so far from us. Oh, I have to tell you something with regard to that. When René and I had come back from the station, Mr. de Montluzin told us that when he heard the train whistle, he turned the* porch (?)[4] *light on and stood there* waving (?) *his white handkerchief until he could no longer see the train.* He said, *"Maybe she could not see me, but I was there anyway!"*[5] *It was very sad, really.*

But I always tell everybody and myself too that we ought to realize how wonderful it was that you could come here *at all and how happy we ought to be that we finally know each other. (And all this is easy to say—but I am as lonely as the others!)* [. . .]

And now I must stop, sending you a heart full of love from each one of us. We can hardly wait for your next letter. I hope you had a wonderful time in Washington. By the way, did you ever remember that you forgot your flowers? I'm enclosing Ada's card in case you want it. Here, too, are the pictures. Isn't the one of Lorraine and Mrs. de M. sweet? And I like so much the ones of you and me! Those were happy days!

Please send our love to your family. Mrs. de M. and I plan to write them soon. René sends you a big kiss, and I, like Papa Delattre, send "a whole Queen Mary" full of them![6]

All my love,
Emily

* * * * *

---

[3] "Good morning, my angel! Good morning, my pink doll! How beautiful you are this morning! Have you slept well?"

[4] Emily inserts in English a few words when she was not sure of the French equivalent.

[5] "Peut-être elle ne pouvait pas me voir, mais j'y étais quand-même!"

[6] Quoting Georges Delattre, Sr., who, in a letter to Arlette while she was in America, had sent her "a whole *Queen Mary* full of kisses."

Bay Saint Louis
September 13, 1948

My dear Arlette,

I have a million things to tell you, and each one wants to be first. I shall tell you a few of them quickly and then return to them for details. Briefly, then, we have had another hurricane, Lorraine is standing, is sitting, and has two teeth, the dolls have arrived, and Mrs. de M. is walking without her crutches! And I have the "flu" and am writing to you as I lie in bed.

Now! I shall go back and elaborate. Last week we had a hurricane, which naturally caused us considerable anxiety, since we remembered the one of last year so vividly. When the radio began to warn us of its approach, everyone made sure there were candles, bread, etc., at home, and many families in Waveland came to the Hotel Reed to spend the night. All night the wind was very strong, but not nearly so strong as last year; and the principal damage was that all the new piers, which were being rebuilt when you were here, were washed away by the high water[. . .]. In fact, every pier from Waveland to Bay St. Louis was destroyed! September is called "the hurricane month," you know, and we all hope we will have no worse storm yet [. . .].

[Emily next reports news of Lorraine, of Venie de Montluzin's continued recovery, of her own attack of influenza, and of the arrival of a shipment of four dolls handmade in France, one of which Arlette wanted Lorraine to have and the others she hoped that Emily could sell for her, keeping the money for future American items Arlette might want to buy.]

I have other news, but first let me say how delighted all of us were to receive the charming letters from your sweet mother, your distinguished papa, and yourself. Every time we find a letter from France in the box at the post office, we feel like celebrating. I am so happy to think that I shall have another beautiful landscape by M. Delattre, and I can hardly wait to build our home to put his paintings into. And all of us are excited over the portrait of Mr. de M. He does not yet know about it. I am always the translator of the letters, which I read aloud at the table, and when I saw those sentences in your letter and your mother's letter, I passed over them, telling René and his mother the good news later. I can imagine Mr. de M.'s surprise when he sees the wonderful portrait. I cannot imagine the happiness one must feel to possess a talent like your father's [. . .].

[Emily continues with numerous brief items of local news, comments concerning recent movies and the Little Theater's new production of *Arsenic and Old Lace*, the family's continued wait for the arrival of a new Pontiac (long-promised by the dealership) and a stretch of bad weather.] It has rained all day today, and a strong wind is blowing over the water, so that the branches of the big oak tree in the front yard are whipping about frantically as I write. Days like this are lonesome days—and I miss my sweet, gay sister more than ever! We still call your two trains "Arlette's trains," and your room, "Arlette's room." Don't give up your plan to return, and the sooner the better!

We shall be sending a box soon. You must be almost out of coffee! (I think of you each time I pour out a spoonful into the sink!) I wish I could taste one of your Mix-Master cakes. Have you made gingerbread yet?

We all follow French politics with keen interest these days.[7] These are surely troublous times for the whole world. (René can hardly wait to find out whether he will receive the flag, but I imagine Gen. de Gaulle is too busy these days!)[8]

Every one of us sends much love to all your family and a big kiss to you. All your friends here have asked me to say they miss you too. Write soon. A heart full of love always,

Emily

* * * * *

---

[7] Within the week and a half before Emily wrote this letter the third ministry of the Fourth Republic (that of the Radical André Marie) had collapsed; the fourth (that of Robert Schuman of the Christian Democrat Popular Republican Movement [MRP]) had been formed, only to survive six days; and the fifth (that of the Radical Henri Queuille) had taken its place.

[8] René had jokingly asked Arlette to ask Charles de Gaulle to send him a French flag when she returned to France. To everybody's amazement she actually wrote to de Gaulle with his request.

[From Georges Delattre, Jr. ("Jojo") to René]

Nogent, October, 1st 1948

My dear René,

  I want you to forgive me for my long delay in writing to you. My sister says I have been lazy for many years but now I shall try to show you I am not lazy anymore.

  First, thank you, Mrs. de Montluzin, for that lovely shirt; I like the shade and the designs. That was exactly what I wished to have and I am glad you guessed my thought.

  And thank you, René, for the delicious chocolate you sent in the first package.

  I should like to know Lorraine, Arlette says she is adorable and when she talks to me in English about Lorraine, she often says, "She is a sugar pie." I have seen the pictures you took of Lorraine, she is a wonderful baby. I hope that all of you are in good health and that Mrs. de Montluzin is completely well and strong. We were so glad to know she is able to walk without crutches. I hope that the flue [sic] of Emily has gone.

  I should like to know the town of Bay St. Louis; Arlette explained to me how beautiful it is. And I know a little New Orléans thanks to her diary. It must be a wonderful town.

  I have been for three weeks in England this summer and I enjoyed very much my trip; Yorkshire is a very beautiful country and I like its very old towns like York.

  Last week I went to Champagne for the vintage near Reims where the famous wine is made. I have been told Charles Boyer likes champagne.[9] I worked one week for vintage with my friends and I was very glad to gather grapes of many vine yards, for it was the first time I did it. I visited cellars in a very great firm of Champagne, they are located at about fifty yards under ground and they are very cool. In these cellars about 1,200,000 bottles of champagne are

---

[9] René had frequently teased Arlette by comparing himself to Charles Boyer. It had become a family joke.

stored. After this I visited some places of the "Battle of the Marne" of the World War I. Today I had my exam of mathematics, physic and chimistry [sic] to pass into the upper class. The black monday is on the forth [sic] of October.[10] In N. Orleans City Guide, Arlette showed me the pictures of Tulane and Loyola Universities where you studied. They look really beautiful.

Arlette told me you make many pretty pictures and I have seen some of them. I like them; she says you are a very good cineast, violonist [sic], and poet. I have read your poetry. My sister says to me that you receive a fine magazine: the *National Geographic* magazine. Would you mind to send me one of them. If it is old it does not matter.

I give my best affectionate regards to all of you.

Sincerely yours,

Jojo

* * * * *

[From Arlette]

Nogent, Oct 2nd, 1948

Dearest Emily,

Exactly like you, when you write to me, I have a million things to tell you. But this time, I write in English (you were a lazy Emily, only 1 and a half line of French in your last letter!). I thank you very much for the pictures, they are really good. I like this one of Mrs. de Montluzin, so distinguished, with our adorable Lorraine. And the other pictures at the swimming pool remind me lovely memories. I am thinking, Lorraine will be soon 7 months old. It makes me sad when you say that I should hardly recognize her now, because I cannot picture her somehow else (*How does one say "autrement"?*) than when I saw her for the last time. I shall look forward eagerly to the pictures of her you will send every month.

---

[10] The day that Jojo would receive the results of his *baccalauréat* examinations, presumably

All of us are very very happy to know at last Mrs. de Montluzin is walking without crutches. I imagine how glad she must be to go around in the house. But you had better to watch how long she stands up when she wants to cook. I remember that Mrs. Crebbin did not want her sister to get tired.

When you wrote there was another hurricane, I did not dare for a moment to go on reading I was so afraid and was fearing Mr. de Montluzin had another heart attack.[11] But so much the better, it was not so serious as last year. Yet, people who had rebuilt their piers are certainly very much disappointed [. . .].

[Arlette here describes her attempts to imitate the voices and gestures of all her Bay St. Louis cousins when her family is at table and discusses her continuing attempts to market her line of handmade doll outfits in America.] This week we sent you a box (by boat) enclosing Mr. de Montluzin's portrait, an oil painting showing the Seine near Notre-Dame, and the little yellow jacket for Lorraine. I knitted it without directions so I fear it will not fit her perfectly. You'll tell me. Next week I shall prepare the rest of what I intended to send you (records, flag). I wrote to Général De Gaulle a few weeks ago, but no answer yet. I hope he will, but you know how busy he is right now,[12] and I have been told that letters addressed to him are very often stolen in the mail services by Communists [. . .].[13]

[She reports discouraging news of her business venture into handmade clothing for dolls. She has only secured one order from a shop in New Orleans, and production costs are proving to be prohibitive.] Did I already write you that I met the buyer of Saks in Paris last month? She gave an order, but when she left Paris she annulled it, telling me the situation was actually too bad in France to

---

[11] René de Montluzin, Sr., had had an attack of angina shortly after Arlette left Bay St. Louis.

[12] De Gaulle was currently in the midst of addressing a series of mass meetings held across France during 1948, meetings overtly appealing to French patriotism and designed to attract supporters for his political bloc, the Rassemblement du Peuple Français (RPF), and for its opposition to both the French Communist Party (PCF) and the ruling "Third Force," the group of center-left and center-right politicians then dominating the Fourth Republic's cabinets.

[13] At the time that Arlette wrote her letter the French Communist Party was in active opposition to the ruling center-left coalition, and insurrectionary strikes and acts of sabotage had erupted across France. Arlette, a committed right-wing Gaullist, would for the rest of her life fear the political power of the French Communist Party.

take orders over here. I don't go any more to my father's office, I work with him at home where I have a typewriter. Maurice told me everything rolled along perfectly without me during three months, and they could go on. So, I prefer to avoid discussions and remain here. Work seems so easy with my sweet Papa. But I am still busy with my two friends who make dolls and dresses. They would like me to help them to sell dolls and new costumes for Carnival Balls. It sounds very interesting.

My dear little Emily, I felt so sorry for you to know you had the 'flu and that you had to be separated for a few days from your darling baby. I hope you recovered quickly. Do your eyes still hurt you?

Wasn't it a surprise for you to receive a letter from Jojo? It is really a shame to have such two lazy brothers, but Jojo would like so much to know "René and his jokes" and all of you that I am sure now he will write very often to be forgiven. He is now taller than me, and I wish you could see how he is a nice boy.

Now, Mrs. de Montluzin you are able to go to the photographer to have a picture made for your portrait. I shall ask you this question until you send the picture, so, you will have soon your four portraits hung up in the hall. And then, this of Lorraine [. . .].

I was glad to read the news about the house remodeled. Bravo, Mr. de Montluzin! I'd like to see how nice it looks now. I hope you have your new Pontiac to take this trip you had planned for Autumn.

Papa is still painting beautiful landscapes and portraits. A very large oil painting of Bellingrath Gardens is now in the living-room. It reminds me a lovely visit [. . .].

My journal is not finished yet, because I decided to add the History of Louisiana in some parts, which I pick up in *N.O. City Guide* and other books. It takes a long time. But I want to have it completely finished so you can read it on Christmas Eve.

My dear Emily, I don't recognize myself. All what I planned to do for my return at home, I gave it up. Do you remember that I told you "Now I'll go out very often," I don't at all; "and I'll change many things in our life," I cannot because of my father who still wants two big meals a day, who does not know how to use Kleenex, but he sings very well *Four Leaf Clover* and *Nature Boy*![14] No more parties like in America, and once again cooking and cleaning dishes and floors! Ah! la, la! Our charwoman does not work, she's been sick for several weeks and she will probably never come back. All the friends I met on the *Queen Mary* are scattered all over the world, I keep a big correspondence with them. When I got home I was still among my recent memories of this trip, but now I realize that all this has gone, you are awfully far away; and I really don't lie when I say that every second of my life is full of thoughts about America. Sometimes I would like to cry, so great are my regrets. And everything here in France right now goes so bad, that we are not any more very proud to be French.[15] Life is so short, it is wasted here by the raise of the prices. I compare every detail with what I saw over there and I don't see any solution to have our country (*relevé*: how do you say this word?). In my mind I think all day long "I want to go back to the States," over and over. But I don't say it aloud. My father would not move. Big problem, I wish I would be still when I was only planning to visit you. Now, I know you, you belong to my life exactly like my father, my mother and my brothers, but between us is this big Ocean. That's why I am lonely very often. It is hard to get rid of happy memories of three months, to think seriously to get used again to France.

Do you have time to read, Emily? I saw *Notorious* and *The Bachelor and the Bobby Soxer* again, we like Cary Grant. I'll get *La Vie En Rose* for you.

If I could beat you, Emily, you wrote you still pour out coffee into the sink! You are terrible! I succeeded in cooking gingerbread exactly like Mrs. de Montluzin's recipe, but using honey instead of corn syrup. That was really delicious and all of them liked it. But it takes plenty of flour and shortening! Does Mrs. de Montluzin still cook her marvelous dishes?

---

[14] The reference is to two of the records of songs popular in America that Arlette had taken back to France.

[15] France during the autumn of 1948 was beset by widespread insurrectionary strikes instigated by the French Communist Party (PCF), which was in political opposition to the current ministry of the Radical Henri Queuille.

Do you hear from your Mother and Harry? Give them my best regards. I write often to all of your friends and relatives. They are lazy to write. Tell me whether René is still joking as usual? I kiss all of you a million times. Please, send often pictures and write soon.

Much love always,
Arlette

P.S. Tell hello to Ernestine[16] and her little boy. Don't forget either all the friends. How many mistakes in this letter?

* * * * *

[From Venie de Montluzin to Arlette's mother, Camille Delattre]

Bay St. Louis, Miss.
Oct. 4, 1948

My dear Cousin,

Thank you for your charming letter. You are entirely too complimentary. It is sweet of you to say so many nice things about me.

They say "seeing is believing." I am afraid Arlette has praised me too highly, and you will have to come and see us, find out for yourself I have been somewhat over rated by your sweet daughter.

Let me say right here we all love Arlette so very much it grieved us for weeks after her departure. I shall never forget how pathetic René, Sr., was when he stood on the porch waving his handkerchief the night she left until the train was out of sight. We all did miss her so much. She is one of those personalities one can not help but love, so charming and genteel, and may I add beautiful. Efficient in every way. We all love her. She definitely must come back to see us. This time we are anticipating your coming with her. In fact, we would like M. Delattre & Jojo to join you. I do not know of anything that would give us more pleasure. René, Sr., as well as all of us would be very happy to meet our cousins

---

[16] Venie de Montluzin's maid

from dear old France. I will assure you we would do all in our power to make your visit an enjoyable one.

Won't you give this a great deal of thought and plan to come?

Let me tell you about our little darling Lorraine. She has grown to be quite a little lady, standing up in her play pen and walking around the sides of it. Too sweet for words.

We think she is beautiful, she has a happy disposition laughing and smiling at all times.

René, Sr., calls her Arlette most of the time.

I am the baby sitter tonight. Emily & René with several couples have gone to Broad Water for dinner and dance. Every time they go out they always say wouldn't it be nice if Arlette was here to go with us.

I am very happy you liked the gifts I sent by Arlette. It is not the intrinsic value, but my love and affection went with them. I am especially glad you liked the little sewing basket. When you come I shall teach you how to make them. They look complicated but really they are very easy to make.[17]

Tell Arlette we now have a nice new porch and steps. After the hurricane [of 1947] our house was a wreck and it took René, Sr., such a long time to make up his mind to have it fixed. Labor is hard to get and prices very high. He is having the drugstore cleaned now & it looks very nice.

Long last I am able to give you some definite news about my hip injury. I went to see my Dr in New Orleans a week ago. He was very much pleased with the X-ray picture and told me I could put away the crutches, which I did immediately. I am now walking with a cane when I go out into the street. Around the house I do not use the cane at all. Strange to say the hip does not pain me in the least, but I do have pain in my ankle & knee caused by lack of exercise, I am sure. When I walk I limp quite a lot. In time that will gradually disappear, I hope. Otherwise I am in excellent health. I am very happy to give you this good news.

---

[17] Venie de Montluzin used long pine needles, which she dyed in various colors and then wove together and shaped into capacious round sewing baskets with close-fitting lids.

René, Sr., like myself is a poor correspondent. Tell M. Delattre he appreciated his letter and says often, I am going to write. I hope some time soon he will do that very thing. I am so happy and pleased about the portrait. We shall ever be grateful to M. Delattre. It is kind of him to go to all the trouble. His work is beautiful and we cherish it very much [. . .].

Very soon Emily & I are going to send a package. In Emily's next letter she will tell you when to expect it. The Drowns[18] had dinner with us today. Olga told us she had gotten a nice letter from Arlette which pleased her very much.

I hope your family will start planning right away to visit us. René, Sr., told Arlette many times how much he would like for the family to visit us. He would have such a good time reminiscing with M. Delattre. He feels so much alone in his French since all his family has passed on and no one in particular to speak to.

I am enclosing some snapshots. Emily has written on the back to tell you about them. Isn't our little Lorraine precious. We shall send more from time to time.

Now that I can get around better I am busy getting the house in order for the winter. I have Ernestine's husband helping me.

Ernestine has been quite sick. We have another maid[19] in her place. We like the new one very much. She is a good cook and one we can depend on every day except Sundays and all holidays. I don't mind for I like to get in the kitchen some times.

Please tell René[20] I received his very nice letter. We enjoyed getting it & hearing from him.

I must bring this to a close. All of us send affectionate greetings to each one of you.

---

[18] René's cousins Richard and Olga Drown, whose two-year-old son had died in 1946 shortly after receiving his vaccination against diphtheria

[19] Venie's new maid Margaret Favre was an accomplished cook, especially of New-Orleans-style Creole dishes. She outlived both Venie and René de Montluzin, Sr., and then worked as a part-time cook for Emily and René, Jr., for decades until she retired.

[20] Arlette's Uncle René, brother of Georges Delattre, who had met René, Sr., and Corinne de Montluzin on one of the family's early trips to France.

I hope to hear from you again soon.

My love to all,
Venie de Montluzin

A big kiss to Arlette.

* * * * *

Bay St. Louis
Oct. 12, 1948

My dear Arlette,

You are right— I am very lazy when it comes to writing in French [. . . , and] this time I'll try to write in French more than usual.

René was very happy to receive a letter from Jojo and will reply soon. We were all enchanted with the letter, really. It's not surprising that you are always so proud of your <u>big</u> <u>little</u> brother. And how handsome he is in the snapshots! It's very evident that in him your mama no longer has a baby!

But <u>your</u> letter, Arlette dear, made us sad. As for me, I've had "the blues" terribly ever since I read it. Here, this summer, you were so gay, so happy, always smiling, laughing, and having a good time, and I am truly grieved when I think of you otherwise. I know that conditions in France at present are deplorable and that all the French who really love their country must be depressed and sometimes nearly without hope; but, Arlette, you must not let yourself become discouraged! There is always the chance with national affairs that suddenly they will be better. I well know that it's easy to say these things, easy to predict better days soon—but in reality there is a lot of truth in the English proverb which says "It's always darkest before the dawn."

Now, as for your work in the house, Arlette Renée Delattre! I am very angry that you stay almost all day long in the kitchen (although it is a very pretty kitchen!). I absolutely want you to "snap out of it" *(Do you know this slang?) and find some friends in Nogent who will make you become once more the same happy Arlette that we knew in Bay Saint Louis. Can't you find another charwoman?*

You are too beautiful and charming to spend all your youth in the kitchen and in front of your typewriter! You tell me that you could whip me because I sometimes throw a little coffee down the sink. Well, I could do the same thing to you because you are letting yourself become a Mademoiselle Hermit! So, in your next letter, I want a report on this problem!

Now, please, may I continue in English? I have so much to say. Thank you!

We were all delighted to know that Mr. de M's portrait and another beautiful landscape are on their way. Your father is too kind and too good to us. We shall be forever in debt to him! It is amazing how quickly he paints, and everything is a real masterpiece, isn't it? I wish I could see the scene from Bellingrath Gardens. We shall look forward to receiving the package and also the one with the French flag and the yellow jacket. Oh, Arlette, you are too sweet to go to so much trouble!

Speaking of packages, I am ashamed to say that only this week I finally mailed the box of summer trousers, shoes, etc., to your mother—you remember, the things I showed you before you left? Maybe your mother can make the trousers fit Jojo or Maurice or M. Delattre for next year. The snow-boots for Jojo are also in the box. I tried to replace the rusty zippers here, but I could not. I am sorry to send them as they are, but they are very warm anyway. Tell Jojo I included four *National Geographic* magazines also and will send others in each box from now on. Some time this week Mrs. de M. and I will mail two other boxes of coffee, flour, etc., and a Christmas gift for each of you. I hope you will like what we're sending. I wish each gift could be much more and that I could step across the Atlantic myself to deliver them! Oh, by the way, in the box of clothes I mailed this week is the pair of nylons Eve Joyce is sending you. I took them out of the envelope they came in and wrapped them in tissue paper—and I did not declare them.[21]

---

[21] Emily had found that if the labels on the packages specifically listed items that were in high demand in France, those items had a considerable likelihood of "disappearing" from the packages as soon as they arrived at the Customs office in France.

Lelette, we <u>loved</u> the pictures you sent. The only thing I am sorry about is how badly the house looked. It really looks nice now. All the little porches are painted too, and the small dining-room also. Why don't you come back and see it again?! We are looking forward to the other pictures, and I'm enclosing a few more we took recently. I wish Lorraine would smile, but the sunlight always makes her frown! [. . .]

René and I took Lorraine to New Orleans recently and had lunch at Mrs. Sporl's.[22] We talked about you the whole time, too! [. . .] [Emily mentions that three of Arlette's dolls have been sold.] Oh, before I forget, Ada asked me to ask you if you would like to have an electric toaster. She has one she never uses and would like to send it to you.

I went to N.O. alone one day last week and bought a black coat and black moiré dress at Godchaux's, two hats (one a black velvet French beret!) at Holmes, and a purse and two pairs of shoes at Maison Blanche. The same clerk at Godchaux's who sold us our dresses sold me the coat, and she asked me at once about you. I have a new red corduroy dress too that I ordered from Macy's (from a picture in *Seventeen* magazine) and I'll enclose a sample to show you. It's <u>really</u> <u>red</u>!

Last week six couples of us went to the Broadwater Beach one night [. . .]. We thought of you and all missed you. Almost every day someone asks me how you are, Arlette. Oh, how much I wish the international situation were not so serious and that you could come back this Christmas! I surely hope your new business with your friends[23] will be <u>very</u> <u>profitable</u> so that you can save a lot of money and return <u>soon</u>. You said America seems far away— I suppose that's because you've crossed the ocean and <u>know</u>! But to me, since I've known you, France seems very near. Anyway, we can all be near you in our letters. I wish you knew how much we miss you!

I'm sure there are many other things to say [. . .]. Please give all our love to your entire family, and especially thank your papa again for his wonderful

---

[22] Ada Sporl, sister of Alice Doll and niece of René, Sr.
[23] Apparently a reference to a new millinery enterprise. See Emily's letter of January 9, 1949.

gifts. Write me often, Arlette, won't you? We miss you so much! René sends you his love, and you know you have mine.

                        Always,
                        Emily

               *   *   *   *   *

                      Bay St. Louis
                      October 25, 1948

Dearest Arlette.

    All English this time. I've so much to say, and it's already late at night! [. . .] [After Emily gives Arlette news of friends and family, she continues:]

    Now, the reasons I delayed writing to you— Ever since Friday Mrs. de M. and I have been preparing the boxes we're sending you all for Christmas [. . .]. Yesterday I mailed the box of gifts, and tomorrow morning I'll mail two boxes of foods, which Mrs. de M is sending. It's necessary now to list each item in the boxes and state how much it cost, so on the box of gifts I deliberately wrote about half-price on some of the articles so that the total value would not be so high. I remembered what you said about Communists in the Post Offices, and I didn't want the box to tempt them by too high a value! I'll tell you what the 2 boxes of food contain, so that you will know whether anything is missing: One box contains 5 pounds of sugar, 3 pounds of shortening, two pounds of coffee, 2 pounds of cheese, 2 cans of syrup, 1 can of chocolate syrup, 1 box of cocoa, 4 packages of Lipton soup-mix, and 1 box of apple pie mix (called "Pye-quick"). The other box contains 2 lbs. coffee, 5 lbs. flour, 3 lbs. rice, 1 can sweet potatoes (to introduce them to your family!), 3 pudding-mix, 1 pancake flour, 1 box of cocoa, and a few packages of chewing gum. We hope everything will reach you safely and in time for Christmas.

Today's news has been good about the 30,000 French soldiers who took possession of the mines without resistance from the Communist strikers![24] I hope the government continues to use force against them!

Arlette, you remember our new Episcopal minister, Mr. Johnson? He and his mother arrived here last Friday, and on Sunday, just before church, he was in his study and lighted a cigarette. Bang! There was a terrible gas explosion and he was badly burned, especially his face and hands. He's in a hospital in New Orleans, where specialists are treating him. They hope there will be no scars on his face, anyhow. Evidently, gas had accumulated in the room from a defective heater [. . .].

I must stop—it's so late! Write us soon, and give our love to everyone in the *Delattre Maison*! René and I are about to drink a Coke. Wish you were here to have one with us.

All my love always,
Emily

* * * * *

Bay St. Louis
November 27, 1948

Ma chère Arlette,

I don't know what to say first! The package has arrived, and your last letter contained wonderful news—and I wish I could speak of both things at the same time!

However, I must choose; and since your letter arrived first, I shall say first of all that we can hardly believe your good fortune at being offered such a wonderful opportunity in New York![25] Oh, Arlette, I do so hope nothing happens

---

[24] French miners had gone on strike on October 7, 1948, as part of widespread insurrectionary work stoppages in support of the French Communist Party (PCF) and its opposition to Henri Queuille's center-left ministry (the fifth ministry since the establishment of the Fourth Republic in January 1947). Queuille called up the army reserves on October 11, and the soldiers subsequently opened up the mine shafts.
[25] See Emily's subsequent letter of January 9, 1949.

to prevent your coming. It would be ideal—even the fact that you could return to Paris twice a year to visit your family has been added to make the whole picture perfect! I have told all your friends here, and everyone is delighted over such good luck for you. You could spend your vacations here with us and in Florida or California, and if we could ever have a vacation, we could go to New York to visit you! Have you made any further plans? Please let us know.

And now about the package! We are all enchanted with the portrait of Mr. de M. It is truly a perfect likeness of him, and it causes us to marvel anew at your father's wonderful talent. When Mr. de M. stands in front of his portrait holding Lorraine in his arms, the baby looks from him to the portrait and back again in great confusion—she sees two grandfathers! My bridge club met here this week, and all the girls thought it was a wonderful resemblance. We cannot thank M. Delattre enough. The portrait itself would have been a superb gift, and when Mrs. de M. saw the beautiful painting of the bridge too,[26] with M. Delattre's charming inscription, she was really overcome with pleasure. What a haunting scene he has painted there! I love your father's style, Arlette. To me a painting should be as real as the scene itself, and I do not care at all for the modernistic cubist or surrealistic style. Do you? Mrs. de M. will write soon to express her gratitude and that of Mr. de M., and in the meantime let me say for them that your father has given this family two more treasures for future generations to love.

Speaking of treasures, Arlette *chèrie*, you gave one yourself when you sent the exquisite yellow sweater for Lorraine. You do beautiful knitting—I wish I were as talented as you. Lorraine is wearing now the pretty blue sweater you made, but I am saving the yellow one until her grandmother and uncle from Dallas come for Christmas. I want her to look especially beautiful then! Thank you, Lelette, *de tout mon coeur*! You are too good to Lorraine.

Speaking of Christmas, will we have your journal to read on Christmas Eve, as you had planned? I can hardly wait to see it. It will help us relive all the happy days you were with us [. . .].

---

[26] Georges Delattre had painted a distant view of Notre Dame at sunset as seen from near one of the bridges over the Seine, with highlights from the setting sun reflected in the water.

Guess what? At last we have the new Pontiac! It arrived last week, and it's dark blue and beautiful. What a pity we did not have it this summer! The next pictures I send you will show how pretty it is. I wish you were here to take some pleasant rides with us.

René and I celebrated our sixth wedding anniversary last Sunday. It was the first one we had had our little sweet Lorraine to be thankful for, and therefore it was a very happy day [. . .].

[More accounts follow of the baby's development at nine months of age, as well as news of the Little Theater's recent presentations of *Arsenic and Old Lace* and *George Washington Slept Here*.]

Isn't the international situation a tragic muddle?[27] I hate to think about it. Were you surprised that Truman was reelected president?[28] Everyone over here was astounded! We saw a newsreel last week showing Communist riots at a ruined French coal mine. And in our own country the dockworkers strike has crippled commerce for weeks. I hope our packages left New York before the strike began. I believe they did.

Arlette, you asked our opinion about whether your family should seriously consider coming to America to live. None of us would like to be responsible for such an important decision, because if unhappiness followed, it would grieve us to think that our advice contributed to it. However, it seems to me that even though times are terrible in France now, M. and Mme Delattre *et Jojo aussi* would be happier living in their own familiar country than in a foreign land where they must begin anew to create a business, a home, and friends. I do not know what to say about Maurice. Perhaps it would be easier for a young man to make such a transfer, and I should think he could obtain work in some printing establishment. But in France you are a family of <u>owners</u> of a business. Would he be contented to be an *employé*? Anyhow, as I said before, such a decision is so important that in

---

[27] At the time that Emily wrote her letter the Berlin Blockade and airlift were continuing; most of eastern Europe was living under repressive Communist Party control; civil war was raging in China, where Manchuria had just fallen (that month) to Mao Zedong's forces; the armies of the newly established State of Israel were still in combat against the five encircling Arab states that had attacked her; and Cold-War tensions were dominating American foreign policy.

[28] Truman had been elected on November 2, 1948.

the end it is you yourselves who will have to weigh everything <u>for</u> it and <u>against</u> it and make your <u>own</u> decisions.

I am afraid I have not expressed myself well in this letter. I have been trying to write it while Lorraine played on the floor at my feet or in her playpen, and of course she has interrupted me continually! [...]

Business is very slow all over town this month, but with Christmas coming, it will improve. We have many beautiful things to sell at the drugstore [...].

Write soon, all about your February plans, and give our love to all your family and special gratitude to M. Delattre.

Je vous embrasse,
Emily

* * * * *

January 1, 1949

Dearest Arlette,

Tomorrow you will be twenty, and our birthday greeting will be several days too late, but it will tell you anyway that we were thinking of you on January 2nd and wishing you much happiness. Are you sorry to leave your "teen-years" behind you? I wonder what your twentieth year will bring you!

As I wrote your father today, we <u>love</u> our portraits! They are wonderful. He is certainly a great artist. I'll write a real letter to you soon.

Love,
Emily

P.S. Thank you for the beautiful Christmas card. Some day we shall see Notre Dame ourselves!

* * * * *

[January 1949 marked not only the milestone of Arlette's twentieth birthday but also the promise of dramatically widening horizons for her in the world of fashion. By that time Emily's time, by contrast, was increasingly taken up with the responsibilities of motherhood, at least while Lorraine was a preschooler, and her letters from 1949 and the first half of 1950 consequently reflect a more settled life for her and her family. Meanwhile, Bay St. Louis continued its steady recovery from the 1947 hurricane, repairing damage to property, effecting improvements, and adding businesses and amenities. For Emily, that tranquil interlude would be abruptly interrupted by the crisis of the Korean War with its attendant national and personal anxieties. For Arlette, the sudden death of her beloved father in 1951 would necessitate her giving up her promising career and devoting herself to the task of helping keep the Delattre family business afloat. (Edit.)]

* * * * *

Bay St. Louis
January 9, 1949

Ma chère Arlette,

Ever since your last letter arrived, I have planned each day to write you; but in the meantime all the Christmas and New Year festivities have occurred, and several other things have happened to keep me so very busy that I couldn't sit down in peace to enjoy writing to my little French sister. Today while Lorraine is taking a nap, I'm beginning your letter; and although I may not finish it until tomorrow, I shall be glad to know that it has at least been started.

First, let me say that we were all distressed to learn that a gift from Mrs. de Montluzin to your father had been stolen from the box you received! It was really the best and most valuable gift in the package—a beautiful pale gray flannel shirt, very light in weight but very warm—something she had hoped he would enjoy for many years to come. It is terrible to think that someone in the [French] customs office must have stolen it. M. Delattre has been so good to all of us in painting our wonderful portraits and landscapes, and Mrs. de M. had wanted him to receive an especially nice gift from her to express her gratitude. Instead, he received nothing but the one white shirt René and I sent! Please tell him how sorry we are. I suppose we should be thankful that nothing else was removed. Were the gifts still wrapped in pretty paper and ribbon? We had tried to make each one look beautiful. We are all so glad all of you liked your gifts and that the food arrived safely. Have you received a box from Lou Tonkel? She told me last week that she had sent a box to you early in November [. . .].

It's wonderful to know that January is already here and that in April you'll be in New York again! It all sounds too good to be true—like a beautiful fairy story. And the owner of the Waldorf is the good fairy who is waving a magic wand! I think it's an excellent idea that you're working some with your friend already so that you can learn about millinery before going to New York [. . .].[29]

[Several paragraphs follow concerning ten-month-old Lorraine's recognition of many words.]

But last week she did a terrible thing! She sat on the floor beside her stroller, placed her little mouth over one of the round iron bars on the side of it, and leaned back so hard that she actually <u>pulled</u> one of her two little lower teeth <u>out</u>! She screamed, and when I picked her up, blood was running down all over her clothes, and her poor little tooth was lying flat against her lower lip! Dr. Ramsey[30] came running to the house when I 'phoned him, and he finished taking the tooth out—it was barely hanging in her mouth! It was a terrible experience, but he is a good dentist, and he says her permanent teeth will not be affected. Now, though, she has only five teeth instead of six! [. . .]

We are worried, however, because there are several cases of scarlet fever in town, and we are keeping Lorraine at home or out only in the car. Beginning today I'm not going to take her for walks, because often people stop to talk to her or touch her.

---

[29] The Paris fashion designer Marie Christiane had just hired Arlette as a model and as a shopping consultant for customers because Arlette spoke English and Spanish as well as French. (She would later add German to her linguistic arsenal.)

[30] The de Montluzins' family dentist, whose office was nearby.

This is inventory time at the drugstore, and every time I have a spare minute, I go down to help René by writing the names of the articles down as he calls them out to me [. . .].

Plans are being made now for the Carnival Ball, which will be held at the end of February. Everyone is trying to guess who the king and queen will be. Almost all of my friends will be attending this year, and all of us are planning our dresses. Mine is to be pale green taffeta made like this: [. . .] [Emily furnishes a hand-drawn sketch of herself in the dress and mentions that the theme of the ball would be "Days of King Arthur."]

January 11th

If I am lucky, some pictures I want to send you will come today and I'll be able to enclose them in this letter. I have a flash-bulb attachment for my camera now, and we tried making some indoor pictures at Christmas. As you'll see, they are too dim. Next time we'll use larger bulbs and turn on all the lights in the room [. . .].

By the way, I told my mother that you had taken your typewriter home from the office of your father, and why—and she said, "Tell Arlette I think she ought to take that typewriter directly back and keep in touch with the business! She should not allow anyone's unpleasantness to drive her away!" So I'm telling you her opinion!

There must be many other things I wanted to tell you, but this letter is almost as long already as your journal. We are certainly eager to see that masterpiece!

Please forgive me for using no French again. Next time I promise I shall! Everyone sends much love to all your family and wishes each one of you the happiest year in 1949 that you've ever had. Write soon.

Te quiero siempre,

Emily

P.S. I had my hair cut yesterday and a new permanent at Ramsey's. It's short, but not too short!

P.P.S. Arlette, do you remember the little old policeman, Mr. Roland Cuevas? He said that he had asked you to try to find out for him if one of his relatives in

France still lives, and just now he saw me and requested that I remind you about this cousin. Her name and address are: Mlle Alice Defosse, 45 rue de Paris, Clichy, Seine, France. She's very old, and he has never received word from her since the end of the war, though he has sent several packages to her. He would appreciate greatly your writing and trying to locate her or at least find out whether she is still living.

* * * * *

[From René de Montluzin, Sr., to Georges Delattre, Sr., dictated in French to Emily, typed by her on the drugstore letterhead stationery, and signed by him]

Bay St. Louis, Miss.
January 12, 1949

My dear cousin Georges,

Better late than never to thank you for the magnificent portrait that we admire every day. *I find that it flatters me a great deal!*

How is everyone? Well, I hope. *Does Arlette still think of giving us a surprise this spring? Her room is ready!*

Lorraine is ten months old today. She is beginning to say some words like "Mama," "Papa," etc. She is very well.

My good memories to the family. While waiting to see all of you with us in America, I send my best regards.

I thank you again for the beautiful portrait.

Love to all,
Your cousin,
René de Montluzin

* * * * *

Bay St. Louis
Jan. 22, 1949

My very dear Arlette,

At last, here are the photos! As you see, they are better than those taken indoors.

It is very late, and I can't write much to you this evening. I don't have any news— Oh, yes, I do! I am now the "production chairman" *of the Little Theater for 1949!* Here are the plays that we are going to have this year:

Comedies:	*Life With Father*
	You Can't Take It With You
	My Sister Eileen
	The Man Who Came To Dinner
Mysteries:	*Love From a Stranger*
	Ten Little Indians

All these plays were very successful on Broadway and in the movies. I think I shall enjoy taking an active part in the Little Theater again.

We are all well and are looking forward to a letter and some pictures from you soon. We have two larger pictures taken at the drugstore to send you and one I've had to send you of Lorraine since last August when she was 4 1/2 months old. In it she looks the way she did when you were here. I am waiting until she is one year old before having a real photograph made for M. Delattre's wonderful portrait-to-be! By that time her hair will be prettier and she will look better in a portrait. I believe soon Mrs. de M. will go to New Orleans and have a photograph made also. We think M. Delattre is like a <u>masculine</u> <u>fairy</u> <u>godmother</u> to be so good to us [. . .].

Love from all of us to you and all your sweet family, Lelette. Please write soon. We miss you.

And I love you!
Emily

And I do, too!
René Jr.

* * * * *

Bay St. Louis
April 9, 1949

Dearest Arlette,

    I wish I could tell you how ashamed I feel when I think how long it has been since I wrote to you last! [. . .] [Emily tells Arlette that her days are filled with caring for Lorraine, who is now walking.] Besides, I try to help René still by keeping his books and making the monthly bills at the drugstore, and I have the big responsibility too of being the chairman of production this year at the Little Theater. That means that, although I have appointed a director for each play, I must be consulted often and go to many rehearsals to be sure everything is being done well. And to add to all this, there's the Bridge Club, you know, and church affairs; and, as you will remember, many parties in this small town! So—I have kept waiting for a day when I would have plenty of time to write you as long a letter as I would like to write—and that day never seems to come! I am at the drugstore now for a little (while Lorraine is at home with her Grandpa and Mamère), and between customers I am at least starting a letter to you.

    This afternoon we darkened one room at home and showed some of our movies [. . .]. One film was the one [. . .] in which you and I were wearing our pretty new dresses just before your tea at the Reed Hotel—you remember that René took our pictures that day? Another film showed Edgar de M.'s visit, and also on the same film were pictures of all of us on Lorraine's christening day. You looked beautiful both times, and seeing you again made us miss you more than ever. And what a difference we could see in Lorraine!

Monday Night

    I had to stop writing Saturday, and since Sunday is always such a full day with us, I waited until tonight to continue:

    Oh, Arlette, there is so much to tell you! First of all, let me say that we are all well and that I'm so sorry my failure to write has caused you to be anxious about us. Your second long, sweet letter made me feel awfully ashamed of myself!

Now about Lorraine [. . .]. [Emily recounts Lorraine's prowess in walking from room to room, her rapidly increasing vocabulary and comprehension of directions spoken to her, and the wide variety of foods that form this one-year-old baby's daily diet.] I would be so happy if you could be here again this summer, Arlette. You would enjoy Lorraine so much more now, because she would be a real little companion. I take her out in the sun now for hours every day, and soon she can play in the sand on the beach near the hotel. You can imagine us there where you used to walk— (I always think of that beach as "Arlette's beach.") It's getting very warm here now. Some people are already going swimming and wearing shorts. Flowers are blooming everywhere [. . .].

Now about the Little Theater: We have presented our first play of 1949, and it was very successful. It was a murder mystery by Agatha Christie called *Ten Little Indians.* The murderer was at last discovered to be Mr. Carter (Charlotte Smith's very charming father!). He and Mrs. Carter gave a party for everyone who had helped to produce the play—at midnight on the night of the last performance. (It was presented for four nights, as is customary for our Little Theater plays.) The next play, the Broadway comedy *My Sister Eileen*, will be given in May [. . .]. Every time I look at the Little Theater, I think of how you put some of that red paint on it! [. . .]

Now for some brief news reports: [. . .] [The postwar Baby Boom continues, with more of Arlette's American friends now expecting.] Bay St. Louis will soon have its own new yacht club, built on that tiny peninsula between Louise Tucker's and Lorraine Camors' houses, where the ruins of an oyster factory still remain. Do you remember the place I am describing? Ramsey's store presented a Style Show at the hotel last week, and I was one of the models! [. . .] It was lots of fun! Mr. Johnson, our minister, is well now, but his hands and one ear are terribly scarred by his burns. Thanks to plastic surgery, his face is not disfigured [. . .]. We went to New Orleans last week to see Mrs. Sporl. She mentioned that [her daughter-in-law] Catherine had received her hat from Paris,[31] but she said nothing about a dress. They must be beautiful, but I am afraid they would be too expensive for me! I have bought several summer dresses in New Orleans recently. I wish you could be with me when I go shopping, as you were last summer! Jojo's plans to go to Sweden or back to England sound wonderful. How I envy him! Sometimes I wonder if we shall really ever see France. But yes, I am determined that we shall! I hope you find a delightful spot to spend your vacation. Probably we shall remain here all summer— It's so hard for René to leave, as you know. He is very happy tonight because of some new records he bought today—Tchaikovsky's Fifth Symphony, a Beethoven concerto, a Rachmaninov concerto, and an album of Gilbert & Sullivan operetta songs.[32] I wish you were here to listen to them with us! Oh, Arlette, we wish for you every day! So many things remind us of you. Lorraine wears her dress you gave her, I use my beautiful purse [. . .], we say "*Magnifique!*"—a thousand things!

I enjoyed reading your article and think many parts of it are very picturesque.[33] Please forgive me for not correcting it immediately. Since this letter will be so heavy, I shall return it when I send the pictures. I hope you will be able to have it published now. I love the sentence "The trees are filled with flowers, and the mocking-bird goes mad with glee." Also, "The groves burst into joyous bloom for Mardi Gras." These are beautiful pictures.

We have seen only a few really good movies recently. *Johnny Belinda, A Letter to Three Wives* and *So Evil, My Love* were excellent. *Johnny Belinda* won for Jane Wyman the Hollywood Oscar for the best feminine acting of the year, you know. *So Evil, My Love* is a British picture with Ray Milland, Ann Todd, and Geraldine Fitzgerald. It's very, very good.

---

[31] Purchased from Arlette's short-lived millinery enterprise

[32] After René was discharged from the Coast Guard, he and Emily decided to use his final Coast Guard pay on an expensive record player and radio combination in a handsome polished wood cabinet. Unfortunately the turntable was designed for 78-rpm records, which within several years were rendered obsolete by Columbia Records' marketing in 1948 of new 33-rpm records.

[33] The article to which Emily refers is the excerpt from Arlette's journal entry about her arrival in Bay St. Louis, which is quoted above. (See "Interlude—Summer, 1948.")

We were delighted with the snapshots of your living room showing M. Delattre and the beautiful picture of a Bellingrath Garden scene. It must be exquisite! Mrs. de M. promises us she will go to Gulfport <u>soon</u> to have her photograph made. I want to wait a little longer for Lorraine's.

I'm so glad you are working with your father at the office again. Bravo! And your work with Christiane must be <u>most</u> <u>interesting</u>. We shall all hope the plans for Fifth Avenue come true!

I <u>must</u> stop! Please give our love to everyone in your family. I wish your whole family could spend this vacation in Bay St. Louis! How we would love to know them!

All my love. Write soon.
Emily

* * * * *

Bay St. Louis, Miss.
May 5, 1949

My dear little Arlette,

A year ago today you arrived in New York—and our thoughts have been with you all day long. In fact, they have been with you for <u>five</u> <u>days</u>, more than usual, because we said on the 30th of April "It was today last year that Arlette left France!" And when this letter arrives at your house, I want it to say to you that our house will be <u>very</u> <u>sad</u> on the tenth of May—

I can't say in French how much we miss you, Arlette, especially now that the weather and the summer season are here to remind us more than ever of your visit with us. You became a part of our life, and it is unthinkable that years should pass without having you with us again. Hasn't the value of the franc increased during the past few months? We have read that it has, and that conditions are much better in France now.[34] I do hope so! The article we read, in

---

[34] The French economy was indeed improving by mid-1949. The plentiful harvest of 1948 had made grain cheaper; the Queuille Ministry's temporary price freeze, imposed in January 1949, had had a stabilizing effect on the economy; national production and consumption were on the rise;

Time Magazine, said that many scarce foods are now available and that you now have electricity all day long. Anyhow, if the franc is now worth more, perhaps you will soon have enough money for another trip—and a longer one this time! We shall never let you go again after only two and a half months!

I am enclosing the pictures I told you I would send. The colored pictures would have been better if we had used a blue flashbulb in our camera. We did not know this, and we used a white bulb. You notice that in two of the pictures we look very suntanned? That is because of the white bulb, it seems! Also, my dress on Lorraine's birthday was rose-colored, not lavender. And her hair looks much too red. It is really a golden-brown with a little hint of red [. . .].

[Emily continues with brief news of the Little Theater and of some of Arlette's friends.] Many piers have been rebuilt, and many new homes built along the beach [. . .]. We are all well, and Lorraine is adorable! She learns new things every day and constantly surprises us. She is very gay and never quiet a moment.

Since this letter is so full of pictures, I shall send your article in a separate envelope in a day or two. Please forgive me for keeping it so long.

René says tell you that on the morning [an error for "afternoon"] of May 10th, when the 6 o'clock train from N.Y. comes in, he will be meeting again in spirit his beautiful blond *cousine* from Paris and seeing her wave a glad "Hello"!

Write soon, Arlette *chèrie,* and give our best love to all your dear family. We want to send a box to you soon. What would be good to include in it? Please tell us.

All my love always,
Emily

* * * * *

---

foods that had been in short supply, particularly meat, eggs, and potatoes, were more readily available, permitting the Ministry to lift rationing of various goods; prices were falling; and consumer confidence was rising. (Dorothy Pickles, *French Politics: The First Years of the Fourth Republic* [London: Royal Institute of International Affairs, 1953; reprint, New York: Russell & Russell, 1971], 106-8.)

[From René Delattre]

July 2, 1949

Dear cousins,

    I am happy to have had news of you, it brings back to me old memories of when Uncle Ludovic and Aunt Reine and my cousin Corine [sic] came to see us in 1889 and in 1900. That wasn't yesterday.

    Arlette brought me the handsome tie that my cousin had the kindness to send to me, and which has given me much pleasure, and I thank you very much.

    My wife and I are back from our vacation on the Côte d'Azur, where I would really like to end my days but alas—

    Receive dear cousins my best wishes and those of my wife. Best wishes also to your family.

René Delattre
284 rue des Pyrénées Paris xx [arrondissement] France

    *   *   *   *   *

Bay St. Louis
July 25, 1949

My dearest Arlette,

    I am sure that you must consider me the laziest correspondent you've ever known. I myself cannot tell at the end of each day why I have been so extremely busy, but it seems as if I never stop a minute. I have read only one book in almost six months, and sometimes I allow almost two weeks to pass before writing to my mother! I hope you never feel as if I am neglecting my *petite soeur* <u>deliberately</u>–– you must always know how much all of us love you and think of you and wish to see you again.

    Of course, my chief occupation these days is Lorraine, and I ought to be <u>triplets</u> to keep up with her. She is the most active little girl imaginable, never quiet a moment, and now at the <u>climbing</u> stage! Every time I look around at her from my work, I find her <u>on</u> <u>a</u> <u>table</u> or trying to climb from a chair onto a dresser! [. . .] [Other examples follow of this newfound activity and Lorraine's growing store of words, including one which Emily knew would delight Arlette's French family: "She can't say 'good,' but she says '*bon*' quite clearly!"]

To tell you the truth, I think you should have come to visit us <u>this</u> summer instead of <u>last</u> summer. Lorraine would have been more pleasure to you now, and, since you left, the house and drugstore have been painted, the Pontiac has arrived, the grass is kept well-cut by René, Jr., with the power lawnmower, and we now have a beautiful new Bendix washing-machine! It's the latest model and entirely automatic. Washing is really a pleasure now! We do it ourselves and have the colored woman come to iron.[35]

I'm enclosing your story, as I would rewrite it for publication in an English paper. Most of the sentences are your own, but occasionally I have changed them a little, as you will see, just to make smoother English. I think you have a real talent for writing, Arlette *chèrie*. Some of your sentences are like poetry—for example, "The mocking-bird goes mad with glee" and "the bushes burst into bloom for Mardi Gras." Those words are beautiful! I hope you will not be angry because I have omitted the page about the de Montluzin family history. It is Mr. de Montluzin's idea that he would prefer not to have it published and that most people would not be interested in it, anyway.[36] I think it was most thoughtful of you to go to the trouble of writing all that, but I know you would want to do what he wishes. Anyway, the article is <u>very good</u> without that page! I added the line about the Little Theater just for fun!

Speaking of the Little Theater, we have presented *My Sister Eileen* and *You Can't Take It with You* since I wrote to you, and next month we will present the famous *Life with Father*. We are ordering the costumes from a large company in Philadelphia which rents costumes to theaters all over America. The costumes will cost us about $170.00 for use for 5 nights, and the royalty on the play (that is, the author's permission to present it) will cost $125.00. The setting has cost

---

[35] Emily in this sentence employs the polite and politically correct term used by the NAACP when it was founded in 1909 and still in use *ca.* 1949.

[36] Arlette's account of the de Montluzin family history was based on her recollection of what René, Sr., had related on her first evening in Bay St. Louis. Part of her account contained errors, a fact that must have powerfully influenced the desire of René, Sr., that that part of the narrative be suppressed.

$40.00, and there are other expenses such as programs, advertising, etc. So you see, we will be lucky if we make expenses on this play! By the way, Effie McCulloch is playing the role of "Mother"—the role Irene Dunne has in the movie. I wish you could be here to see it! We wished for you last Saturday, too. The Little Theater had another barbecue just like the one last year, remember? This time we arrived not quite so late!

Arlette, we have not forgotten about the stockings, but we haven't sent them because we wanted to ask you if it is safe to send them in a box stating that the contents are nylon stockings. Would such a box be stolen at the customs office now, as in former days? Should we send one stocking at a time in letters, as you did last summer? Please let us know. Would you like some Kleenex?

Before I forget, please ask M. Delattre if he would consider painting a portrait similar to ours for a friend of Mrs. de M's who wishes a portrait of her son. The boy is about fifteen years old, and she would send a photograph, of course. If he would paint the portrait, will you please tell me how much he would charge for it. (Do not charge <u>less</u> than $150.00—that is <u>my</u> opinion! Such portraits are worth <u>much</u> more than that!) [. . .]

We have been thinking of Jojo and hoping that he succeeded admirably in his examination[37] and had a good vacation in England [. . .].

You mentioned seeing crowds of American tourists in Paris. Every New Orleans newspaper shows pictures of happy groups about to sail for Europe, and we envy every one of them! But we are determined that <u>we</u> <u>will</u> <u>come</u> too, and our only regret is that it seems impossible <u>now</u>.

How interesting your work with Christiane must be! And how impressive it sounds that you are *"la vendeuse-interprète en anglais et espagnol"*![38] Do you think Christiane still plans to open her Fifth Avenue shop this fall? We are so eager to see you again. We looked at the movies last night and there you were, looking very beautiful! I am glad you reminded us about the copy of the film. I shall try to get one for you.

---

[37] Georges, Jr., had recently taken his *baccalauréat* examination.
[38] A personal shopper fluent in English and Spanish

Yes, I have added many pictures and many words to Lorraine's book. In fact, it's now finished, and I must start another.

The one book I have read recently is *Dinner at Antoine's*. René is reading it now, a little each night, and he can hardly put it aside! It's very exciting and fascinating. As for movies, we enjoyed *Flamingo Road* very much, also *Enchantment*. I remember well *Since You Went Away*. It was good, wasn't it?

Mrs. de M., René, and René, Sr., join me in sending our best greetings to your mother, your father, and Jojo, and for you a special hug and kiss from all of us! Write us soon.

Lots of love always,
Emily

* * * * *

Bay St. Louis
September 16, 1949

My dear little sister Arlette,

It seems that I am developing a habit of beginning every letter with an apology for my long delay in writing—but, really, Arlette, since Lorraine is at the <u>running</u> and <u>climbing</u> and <u>investigating</u> stage, you have no idea how <u>completely</u> she occupies my time all day long! [. . .]

Oh, Arlette, your last letter was one of the most interesting ones you've ever written! You must have a wonderful time working for Christiane! How nice to meet pleasant people at luxurious hotels and help them to go shopping—and how pleased your parents must be, since they wanted you to develop poise and assurance! (Of course, it seemed to all of us as if you were <u>already</u> the most poised young lady in the world!) Be sure to tell me more about Mr. Kossoff. Surely, with all the American contacts you are making, and with the money you are saving, you will be able to return to the States soon! You have many friends here who would be so happy to see you again. Very often, even now, people ask me about you or mention something you said or did while you were here. <u>Everybody</u> wants you to come back!

Before I forget, let me tell you that I sent the check for $16.00 to Jacqueline[39] and received a very nice note from her in acknowledgment of it. Since you said her package had been opened by robbers, I have hesitated about sending the stockings, especially since I ought to declare them on the customs tags. If you want me to take the chance and try to send them anyway, however, I shall do so [. . .].

At last work is being done to repair the beach road! We have new city commissioners, who apparently are honest and are using city funds for the public good. All the road has now been filled in and widened wherever the hurricane had destroyed it, and as soon as the fill has settled, the new road will be paved. When you come back, you will see many new homes and businesses—even a drive-in, open-air theater!

The Little Theater has had another big success—*Life with Father*—and in three weeks more it will present *Rebecca*. (Adaline Samuel, who is directing it, 'phoned me tonight that her doctor told her today that she has heart trouble and must go to bed for two weeks at once! Now I must find a substitute director before the next rehearsal, this Monday!) The play following *Rebecca* will be *The Man Who Came to Dinner*, to be directed by Mrs. Blair. The cast has already been selected and Mrs. Blair will begin rehearsals before *Rebecca* is presented. Her play will be the last of the year, and I shall be very glad! It has been a great responsibility and has required too much of my time. However, every play so far has been excellent, and the Little Theater's reputation has grown considerably, so I suppose it has all been worth the effort!

Believe it or not, Mrs. de M. went to New Orleans and had her photograph made at Holmes a few days ago! I hope she will be pleased with it so that she can send it to M. Delattre. It is so wonderful of him to offer to paint her portrait, and I know that some day Lorraine will be very proud to have portraits of her parents and grandparents, made in France! [. . .]

---

[39] Jacqueline Fiola, Arlette's childhood friend in South Nyack, who had been serving as an intermediary in her continued efforts to market handmade clothing for specialty dolls in America

My mother and Harry spent a week in August with us, arriving on the night of my birthday. It was wonderful to have them here. Isn't it a shame for families to be separated by so many miles?

We hope M. and Mme Delattre and Jojo enjoyed their vacation trip. I imagine, judging from your letter, that you decided not to go. Jojo must be in school again now. I know all of you are very proud of him!

Everyone here sends a heart full of love to you and your mother, father, and Jojo. Write me soon.

All my love always,
Emily

*   *   *   *   *

Monday Night
November 14, 1949

My dear "Lelette,"

It is already late, and I should not begin your letter tonight, I know. But, even if it is not a long one, I wanted to write a letter in order to enclose this newspaper clipping, which appeared in the Gulfport *Herald* a few days ago, and this invitation,[40] which we received yesterday [. . .].

We are all so enchanted with everything you tell us about your work at Christiane's! Do you know the fairy story about Cinderella, a beautiful blonde whose fairy godmother transported her from the kitchen of her home to the gaiety of a royal ballroom? You remind me of her— Christiane is the fairy godmother, and I'm sure the royal ballroom could not compare in brilliance and excitement to the world of fashion you now live in. I wish I could see you modeling lovely fur coats and hats! And I just can't imagine you with your hair cut very short! Please be sure to send us some snapshots. <u>My</u> hair is shorter, but not <u>very</u> short yet. I

---

[40] An invitation to the wedding of one of Arlette's frequent "dates" of the preceding summer in Bay St. Louis

am not as bold as you are in taking the fatal step— I must attain short curls by degrees! [. . .]

[Emily sends good wishes to Maurice and Huguette, whose second baby is due soon and who had lost their first one; and she reports the latest news of Lorraine.]

Have you finished *And Now Tomorrow*? I liked it, but I liked *All This and Heaven Too* better. Rachel Field is one of our best contemporary writers, in my opinion.

We are looking forward to seeing your great French movie *Monsieur Vincent*[41] this week. It will be the first time Bay St. Louis has ever presented a foreign movie (except English ones). The preview looked marvelous [. . .].

René and I drove in to New Orleans last Saturday to see a big football game between Tulane University and the U.S. Naval Academy. Afterwards we had dinner at Arnaud's. It was fun—we seldom get away together alone nowadays!

We have almost completed a small package which we will send soon— probably by airmail—so that it will reach you and your family by Christmas. However, I'll write again in the meantime to wish all of you happy holidays. Everyone here is well and sends much love to you all.

I embrace you,
Emily

* * * * *

Bay St. Louis
March 9, 1950

My dear Arlette,

When I wrote "March 9" a moment ago and realized that I am only now writing to thank you for gifts received at Christmas, I felt like hanging my head in

---

[41] A 1948 French-language film about the life of St. Vincent de Paul.

shame. I believe that you will forgive me, though, when you hear some of the things that have been happening here [. . .].

[As well as expressing thanks for the Christmas gifts, Emily discusses plans for a birthday party for Lorraine to which she has invited fourteen children, their mothers, and all Lorraine's aunts from New Orleans. She tells Arlette of the singing, drawing, and use of French phrases the two-year-old is astonishing the family with, and as usual she adds news items concerning various friends in Bay St. Louis.] A terrible thing happened this weekend: You remember [. . .] [a young man Arlette had briefly dated]. His older sister, Cynthia, was expecting her first baby this week and was apparently in perfect health; but last Saturday night she awoke with a violent headache and almost immediately lost consciousness; and about half an hour later, in an ambulance on the way to New Orleans to a hospital, she died! It was a cerebral hemorrhage, the doctor said later. Anyway, he instructed the ambulance driver to turn back to Bay St. Louis so that he could take her body to our little hospital[42] and try to save the baby. The poor little baby—a beautiful little girl—lived six hours and then died too. They were buried together—the saddest funeral you can imagine.

But let me speak of happier things. You asked how we spent New Year's Eve. We had the best time we've had in <u>years</u>, Arlette! Our new Yacht Club[43] opened that night, and after going to a party first at Adaline Samuels', we joined a group of our friends at the Yacht Club and stayed almost all night! It was the

---

[42] The only medical facility in Bay St. Louis in 1950 continued to be King's Daughters Hospital, a small cottage clinic. It had no operating room or sophisticated equipment, and most patients in need of emergency care for serious conditions had little choice but to travel by ambulance, with a doctor in attendance, some sixty miles to New Orleans, as Venie had done when she broke her hip. Traveling east to a closer hospital in Gulfport was impossible, since the automobile bridge over the Bay of St. Louis, destroyed in the 1947 hurricane, had still not been rebuilt. Emily with great excitement would tell Arlette in a letter of May 19, 1950, "Bay St. Louis is going to have a new bridge at last! A <u>four-lane</u> <u>concrete</u> bridge, to be begun as soon as the state and federal government decide exactly where to build it." Until its completion drivers heading east from Bay St. Louis had no alternative to traveling a long distance by narrow back roads around the entire perimeter of the bay.

[43] The Bay-Waveland Yacht Club was the brainchild of John and Mary Cannon Bell, the same postwar newcomers to Bay St. Louis who had spearheaded the creation of the Little Theater and who would soon be instrumental in the establishment of a golf club in Pass Christian on the opposite side of the Bay of St. Louis.

most gala event Bay St. Louis has had in along time! Carnival was fun this year, too. Mother and Harry came to spend a week with us, and we enjoyed their visit so much. René and I took part in the Carnival Ball again this year and attended the King's supper-dance at the Yacht Club afterwards and the Queen's cocktail party at the Reed the following day. We're going in to New Orleans next week to see the musical *Oklahoma!*, and on Easter Sunday we are both going to be in a wedding [. . .].

But all our activities are mild and colorless compared with yours! Imagine visiting London, and going out with attachés of this embassy and that, and modeling fabulous fur coats, and contemplating a trip to Spain! Your letters are as exciting as a novel! Write us more, and write soon!

Please give our love to all the family. We are anxious to hear about Maurice and Huguette's baby. We do so hope it arrived safely and will bring them much happiness. Try to find time to write us soon, and forgive me for waiting so long!

All my love as ever,
Emily

P.S. I haven't had time to read much lately, but René has read and enjoyed *The Vixens* by Frank Yerby and *Brief Gaudy Hour*, a biography of Anne Boleyn. The best movie lately is Olivia de Havilland's *The Heiress*.

* * * * *

Bay St. Louis
April 13, 1950

Dearest Arlette,

Isn't it strange how often our letters cross each other in flight? Frequently when I write to you, I have the impression that you are writing to me at the same time—and sure enough, about the day I expect you to receive my letter, I find one from you in our post office box! I believe that sometimes we must establish some sort of thought-transference, even across the wide Atlantic.

Let me tell you first of all that the lovely handkerchiefs arrived for René and Mr. de M. and that they were both delighted to receive them. One does not find such exquisite workmanship in America. They asked me to thank you for them, since they are both very good at <u>intending</u> to write and very <u>bad</u> at actually <u>doing</u> it!

At long last I have a very good photograph of Mrs. de M. ready for mailing, and I'll mail it *par avion* at the same time I send this letter. Please call M. Delattre's attention to the fact that her glasses are not exactly straight. They are a little too far down over one eye, but when M. Delattre paints the portrait, I know he will be able to correct this small detail. One sleeve of her blouse is wrinkled, too, but that also can be attended to, I am sure. I hope he likes the photograph as much as we do. We think he is so wonderfully good to us to make <u>four</u> marvelous portraits, and we shall never finish being grateful to him. Tell him if he does not think the shade of her blouse is pretty, he will make it any color he chooses, we hope. Since her eyes are blue, she wore a blue blouse that day, but I think perhaps the photographer tinted it too light a shade. Anyway, M. Delattre will know best.

I have some news for you that is both bad and good. Mr. de M. had a very serious heart attack about one month ago—just a day or so after I wrote you my last letter—but he is now well again and three days ago went back to the drugstore. Of course, he realizes now that he must be very careful about not overexerting. For a week after his attack, the doctors would not even allow him to feed himself! He feels well again now, though, and he is much happier at the drugstore doing light work than he is at home being idle.

René and I were in a wedding at our little church on Easter night. The bride was a new friend who came here to live only six months ago, and the groom is from Pennsylvania. I was the bride's matron-of-honor, and René was a groomsman. I'm enclosing a piece of material from my dress. The other two bridesmaids wore dresses of the same tissue faille, but light green in color. Their bouquets were yellow, and mine was flame-colored. The men wore full-dress suits, and you should have seen how handsome and gracious your cousin René looked! (Naturally, I'm prejudiced in his favor, but he really <u>did</u> look good!)

After the wedding there was a reception at the Yacht Club, where champagne was at our elbows constantly, and where the music was supplied by a pianist and a violinist who came to New Orleans from Paris only two months ago to study at the Loyola School of Music!

We thought of all of you at Easter and hoped you had a happy holiday. I know having little Dorothée in the family now makes every day a happy one. We have a little gift for her, which I'll mail in a few days. We are all so glad she arrived safely and that Huguette is well again. Isn't it wonderful how much joy a baby can bring into a family? When you take some pictures, try to send us one of her too. Please congratulate Maurice and Huguette for us. I'd like to send them a card of congratulations, but I don't have their address [. . .].

[Here follows a report on Lorraine's new accomplishments of singing many songs, including *Frère Jacques* in French, and of talking to Emily's mother on the telephone. As usual, Emily adds news about Arlette's Bay St. Louis friends.] [. . .]

How wonderful it would be if we could tell everyone that you were coming back this summer—and for more than three months this time! Is passage as expensive now as it was when you came two years ago? In a way, I'll hate to read your journal when it comes, because I know it will make us all very lonely for you.

I hope everyone is well *at the Delattre home* (the only French I've written in this whole letter! *How lazy I am!)* All our family sends much love to you all, and Lorraine (with my help, of course) has a message for you:

I love you, Arlette!
Lorraine[44]

Me too!
Emily

---

[44] Written in French with a fountain pen and with Emily guiding Lorraine's hand

P.S.   We are having a new floor of black and white asphalt tile put down in the drugstore and many shelves repainted. You should come back to see how nice it looks!

* * * * *

Bay St. Louis
July 25, 1950

My dear Arlette,

So much to enclose in this letter that I shall try to write all I have to say on this page alone.

We were all enchanted with your lovely snapshots. You are so slim and *élégante,* so poised and stylish! And what an *artiste* Mme Delattre is with her needle—she rivals in her own art your father and his brush! Jojo is so tall and handsome—and, suddenly, a young man, Arlette. Someone I showed the pictures to asked me if he were your boyfriend! But as for you yourself, you must have lost some weight, haven't you? You look very slender, and it's very becoming. I notice you are wearing your pearls[45] in some of the pictures. We're so glad you're really enjoying them. Your short hair is quite *chic*—altogether you look just as charming as any of the models in the <u>beautiful</u> fashion magazine you sent! It's hard to tell which dress I like best. Who took the picture of you in the pink linen suit? The effect of the dogs and the beautiful car is that of a professional photographer. I am showing all four pictures to many of your friends here, and you can imagine how delighted they are to see them.

The magazine arrived yesterday and we have been poring over it ever since. Thank you for all the pleasure it will give us and the friends I intend to lend it to. Marie Christiane's hats look exquisite. But what <u>astonished</u> me was the white organdy stole edged with white <u>fox</u>! What an idea! But it must be absolutely breathtaking [. . .].

---

[45] A gift from René and Emily

Now, Arlette, you must sit down and tell me much more about [. . . J. ———]⁴⁶! Describe him in great detail, and tell me how you feel about him! The little scraps of information you have mentioned sound very, very interesting, and we want to know more. *Immediately!* And how gorgeous your dresses and his furs must have been!

René asked me to tell you that he has instructed the *Sea Coast Echo* office to send you the *Echo* every week. He thought perhaps you'd like to glance at it and see what your friends here are doing. By the way, we now have a television set, a wonderful RCA 16-inch-screen set! The first night we turned it on, we saw the July 14th parade you described, the president and all![47] What a miracle of science television is! [. . .]

Lorraine is going to her first movie tonight! We are taking her to see *Cinderella*, the Walt Disney technicolor picture. She already knows the story well and even all the music, so I think she will love the picture.

A thousand kisses to all of you!
Write soon!
Emily

P.S. About Korea—I won't try to say how we feel. It would take pages.[48]

*   *   *   *   *

---

[46] Arlette's new friend, a British furrier, who seemed to be developing romantic feelings for her and who will in upcoming correspondence be referred to in this way

[47] Emily refers to the Bastille Day parade in Paris and to Vincent Auriol, member of the French Socialist Party, wartime Resistance worker, and (1947-54) first President of the Fourth Republic.

[48] North Korean armed forces had crossed the 38th parallel and invaded South Korea on June 25, 1950, one month before Emily wrote this letter. During that one month the United Nations Security Council had passed Resolution 83 calling upon the U.N.'s members to assist South Korea militarily; President Truman had committed American forces to the fight; large numbers of South Korean soldiers had fallen back in the face of the invading North Korean Army or defected to the North; the U.S. Air Force had sustained heavy losses; and American and South Korean Army units were retreating to Pusan, leaving most of South Korea for the moment in North Korean hands.

[From Venie de Montluzin]

Bay St. Louis, Mississippi
Aug. 20/50

Dear Monsieur Delattre,

My portrait has arrived in first class order, and as I look upon each portrait you have so generously made for us words are not fully sufficient to express our love and gratitude to you for so many wonderful treasures you have given us. We will enjoy and cherish them all our lives.

Monsieur Delattre, each one in itself is so wonderfully done! When we consider the time and patience you have so willingly given, we would love to embrace you and say *"Thank you with all my heart!"* Couldn't you and Madame Delattre come to visit us and make that possible? It would give us great joy to have you. We would do everything in our power to make your visit a pleasant one.

It is a pity that you and René could not have met years ago. He loved his family and it makes him very sad to know he is the last one left from rather a large family. He is very well and still goes to the store every day.

The last pictures of Arlette are beautiful. It has been a privilege to know and love her.

Jojo has grown tall and quite handsome. When you and Madame Delattre come to see us, you must by all means bring him along too. Your little granddaughter, I know, is a source of joy and happiness to the whole family, like our dear little Lorraine.

Lorraine is quite a singer. She knows ever so many songs, and it is surprising how she can carry a tune.

Thank you again, dear Monsieur Delattre, for all the wonderful gifts you have given us.

All of us send affectionate greetings to you and each member of your family.

Fondly and sincerely,
Venie de Montluzin

* * * * *

Bay St. Louis, Miss.
September 19, 1950

Arlette *chèrie*,

Please forgive me for waiting almost two months to write you. As usual, my days have been very full and entirely too short to do all I would like to do. I'll tell you more about what I've been doing later.

In fact, I'm <u>bursting</u> with news items for you this time! But the first thing I want to talk with you about is the [. . . J. ——] situation. René and I have been worried about you ever since we read your last letter—because we both noticed the same thing in your account of Mr. [. . . J. ——]: you described him very casually, you mentioned the possibility of marriage very coldly, and you never used the word "<u>love</u>" a single time! Now, Arlette, you must listen to your big sister and brother! It may be very naïve to insist that love is the best foundation for a happy marriage—but without doubt this is true. And from all you told us about his eccentricities, <u>I</u> <u>hope</u> <u>you</u> <u>will</u> <u>not</u> <u>marry</u> <u>him</u>! No doubt he has been a pleasant and valuable friend, but he does not sound like good <u>husband</u> <u>material</u>! You are at the peak of your youth and charm, and you deserve a husband who never divides his love for you with his love for fur coats! And you should marry a Frenchman, I think—or an American! At any rate, we are very anxious to hear the next chapter of your story; so please write us soon! How do your parents like [. . . J. ——]? By the way, what <u>is</u> his first name? [. . .]

Did M. Delattre receive Mrs. de M.'s recent letter? I can't begin to tell you how delighted we are with her portrait! He has caught her dignity and her sweetness perfectly—and the coloring is exactly right. I marvel every day at his wonderful talent—for instance, the luster on each of the pearls in Mrs. de M.'s necklace is so realistic one is inclined to touch them to be sure they are only canvas and paint! It must give an artist much joy to create such lovely things [. . .].

Oh, Arlette, we had a very frightening experience on August 30th! Let me tell you about it. On August 25th the radio and newspapers told us that a small hurricane was beginning to form in the Gulf of Mexico. Each day it became larger and stronger, and each day it approached closer to New Orleans, but always there was the hope that it would turn and change its course to another direction. But on the morning of the 30th the announcement was made that only a miracle could save New Orleans and the whole Gulf Coast, because the hurricane was very large by then and very strong, and we were directly in its path! All day the radio repeated its warnings: "Hurricane winds of 160 miles per hour, extremely high tidal waves, and more destruction of life and property than ever before are expected. Take every precaution! The hurricane will strike New Orleans about 7:30 tonight and the Gulf Coast about 8 tonight! Leave your home if you live on low land!" Well, you can imagine how heartsick everyone was! All over the Coast and in N.O. there was the sound of hammering, as people nailed wooden boards across their windows and storefronts. Everyone bought candles and filled containers with water, in case electricity and water supply were cut off, as they were in 1947. The grocery stores sold canned food all day long, and people who lived on streets where water was high before worked all day building supports on which they could place their furniture a few feet higher than the floor. Many families took rooms at the Reed Hotel for the night. We (our family) felt as if we were safe, since this house is strongly built and on high land; so we stayed here. All afternoon the wind increased in strength, and all anyone could do was wait—wait—wait! As we ate our supper at 6:30 the wind began to howl and shriek, and we said to ourselves, "Well, here it comes!" And I'll admit we were all afraid—not only for ourselves, our home, our drugstore—but for our friends and our beautiful Coast which lay waiting helplessly. But then the miracle did happen! Just at 7 o'clock the wind suddenly stopped. We went out on the porch and saw that the rain had stopped, too, and the moon and stars were shining. We could hardly believe it and still don't understand exactly what happened. According to the weather bureau, the hurricane mysteriously turned like this, just before its full strength reached the Coast and the city. [Emily drew a small sketch to illustrate the 90-degree angle at which the hurricane turned and headed back out to sea just before it reached New Orleans. (Edit.)] They say such a thing has never happened before. It was almost like turning off an electric light—one moment there was wind & rain; the next moment calmness and bright stars! And think of the work the next day to put furniture back into place and remove boards from windows! [. . .]

I know all of you must be following the war in Korea as anxiously as we are. The news is much better now, of course,[49] but where will the whole terrible world-situation end? Already there is a new crisis in Indo-China.[50] I hate to think what the future may hold for our generation and our children all over the world. Here we feel really at war again. Every day the radio reports lists of Louisiana and Mississippi boys wounded, killed, or missing in Korea. All day and night trains rumble through our little town carrying soldiers, tanks, army trucks, airplanes, jeeps, etc., to New Orleans. One day we counted seven long trains within one hour! Some people are hoarding, but not very many, I believe. Let us know if ever you need certain foods or other articles again in Paris. You know we would be so glad to help you get them. We hope that René and Harry will not have to go to war again, but we expect René's cousin in California to be called by the Marines again at any time. Mrs. Crebbin and Miss Word[51] are in California now spending 3 weeks with him. He is like a son to them.

I've been helping our newly organized "League of Women Voters" here to make a survey of our town's government, educational facilities, etc., and I've been very busy. There have been the usual parties, too—many of them at the Yacht Club. So often we talk of you at those parties, and I tell the latest news of you.

---

[49] On September 15, 1950, Douglas MacArthur had launched his successful amphibious landing at Inchon. Over the next several weeks American forces, together with their U.N. allies, had broken out of Pusan, retaken Seoul, and driven the North Koreans before them. American and South Korean armies would cross the 38th Parallel into the North in early October 1950.

[50] French military forces in Indochina suffered a humiliating series of defeats at the hands of the Vietminh in the autumn of 1950, with Dong Khé falling in September. What appeared to be the danger of a French rout would be alleviated over the next several months after General Jean Joseph Marie Gabriel de Lattre de Tassigny assumed personal command and drove back the Vietminh, who reverted to guerrilla tactics.

[51] Two of Venie de Montluzin's sisters

We are all well. René has watched his diet carefully for 3 months and has lost 22 pounds! He looks very handsome, I think, & feels younger & better.

I don't like to go on to Page 11, though I could, easily! Please give our love to all your family and write again soon, especially about [. . . J. ——]!

All our love always,
Emily

* * * * *

Bay St. Louis, Miss.
November 11, 1950

Ma chère Arlette,

I have been trying to write to you for weeks, but I am glad, in a way, that I have waited, because I have many more things to tell you now!

First, however, I want to say how much happier we feel about [. . . J. ——] since you told us so many more details about him! He sounds exceptionally attractive and admirable, and I hereby withdraw all the doubts I expressed about him in my last letter! Seriously, I don't feel as if the difference in your ages is as great as it sounds. You are as mature as you will ever be, don't you think? And he is probably younger and more full of "*la joie de vivre*" than most men of forty. Remember how immature and boring you found the American boys your own age?[52] I think you would be happier with a man who is considerably older than you; and, after all, forty is still quite young! At least, that is what René and I think. René was forty in September, and he is by no means old! You and Mr. [. . . J. ——] have another tremendous advantage in the fact that you both are a part of the same world of fashion. It seems to me as if any man in whom you are seriously interested would be very grateful for such good fortune. You are all a husband could want, I am sure, and I think [. . . J. ——] is a very lucky man. He must be a very clear-thinking and discerning man, too, since he has evidently

---

[52] Arlette had told Emily on her visit in 1948 that the conversation of most of the young American men she dated in Bay St. Louis consisted almost entirely of talk about sports.

pushed aside all the flattering, hypocritical women you mentioned who constantly surround him and has shown his preference for a certain Mlle Delattre whose good breeding, intelligence, charm, and sincerity are so obvious! I feel like saying "Bless you, my children!" I hope your next letter will tell us that your engagement is definite. If you marry him, will you have to spend most of your time in England? That would be a pity—though perhaps England is pleasanter than you think.

Incidentally we all shuddered when we read of the crash of the Paris-to-London plane last month. Thank goodness neither you nor he was on it! You and Christiane must have had a wonderful trip to London that time with all your hats– –and with such an attentive host! [. . .]

[Emily comments on her continuing efforts to have a good photograph taken of Lorraine for the portrait Arlette's father had offered to paint, and she discusses at length Lorraine's latest activities.]

I mailed on November 9th our box of Christmas gifts for all of you. Hope it arrives in time for Christmas. We sent it with much love for each one of you and with the wish that by <u>next</u> Christmas we may see you again somehow. In case something may disappear at the Customs Office, I think I'll tell you, as I did last year, the contents of the package, so that you will know if anything is missing. (Of course, you can read this to your family or not, as you prefer!) For Jojo—pajamas; for Mme Delattre, 3 pairs of nylon hose; for M. Delattre, cuff links and a tie clasp; for Dorothée, a silver spoon and fork; and for yourself, something very pretty in white nylon which we hope you'll wear on your honeymoon! [. . .]

Did I tell you in my last letter that René and I went to New Orleans to see the Sadler's Wells ballet present *Swan Lake*?[53] It was a never-to-be-forgotten treat. We went to a very amusing costume party at the Yacht Club last week too– –a Shipwreck Party, where the costumes represented anything nautical or South Sea Island-ish! Lorraine Camors won the prize for the best woman's costume. She was dressed like a Hawaiian girl, grass skirt and all. Last night we saw the

---

[53] Margot Fonteyn was the *prima ballerina* in the performance.

Little Theater's last play of 1950—a very clever comedy about the French settlers of Louisiana.[54]

I've read a particularly good novel this week—*The King's Cavalier*, by Samuel Shellabarger. The setting is France in 1523, and the story is so well done that I closed the book with real regret.

I went to New Orleans a few weeks ago with Iva May McDonald and Lorraine Camors, and bought for myself a pretty dark-brown wool-gabardine suit and a red velour hat. We're going to a cocktail party next week, and I'll wear them for the first time. Oh, I was forgetting to tell you that Margaret Shadoin, Ada Whitfield, and I gave a big morning coffee party 2 weeks ago at Ada's house in honor of a friend who had just married. We invited 136 guests! Wish you could have been with us!

Please give all your family our love and kiss Dorothée for us. Write when you can—your letters are big events for us! Everyone sends love to you, *and I send you a big hug,*

Emily

*   *   *   *   *

Bay St. Louis, Miss.
December 5, 1950

Arlette dearest,

Just a note to say, in a more personal way than a card can say, that all of us wish all of you a very happy Christmas season—at least, as happy a Christmas as is possible under the shadow of present world affairs.[55] I feel as if our

---

[54] *The Great Big Doorstep*

[55] In late November 1950, a confident MacArthur had launched a military offensive intended to bring an end to the fighting in Korea by year's end, only to be met immediately by an enemy counteroffensive joined by over a quarter of a million invading Chinese. Within days, American and other U.N. forces were in desperate retreat in frigid winter conditions, fighting for their lives and sustaining heavy casualties. Truman in mid-December would issue a presidential proclamation declaring a state of national emergency. A new enemy push, the Chinese New Year's Offensive, would result in a further U.N. fallback culminating in early January 1951 in the capture of Seoul by the Chinese and the North Koreans.

generation's way of life is rushing toward a waterfall, like a small boat unable to help itself. Certainly tremendous changes are coming all over the world, even if, by a miracle, diplomatic maneuvers should forestall an immediate world war.[56] But let's not think too much of these gloomy matters at Christmas time, if we can prevent it.

Thank you so much for Lorraine's two adorable dolls and my lovely scarf [. . .].

I hope you've received the box of Christmas gifts we sent—and I hope everything is still there! Did you ever receive Dorothée's little silver dish? I'm afraid it was lost again.

Lorraine is looking forward to Christmas so eagerly and sings Christmas songs all day long. She can be heard all over the house! Santa Claus is going to bring her a big red tricycle, which she is sure to enjoy for two or three years. Wish all of you could be with us to celebrate. Mother and Harry will be here. Will [. . . J. ——] spend the holidays in England or in France?

Please wish all your family a merry Christmas from all of us. We will be thinking of you.

Much love always,
Emily

P.S.   *La Vie en Rose* is at last to be heard on all sides over here. Every juke box & radio program plays it now, and we always smile and say, "Listen! There's Arlette's song!"

*   *   *   *   *

---

[56] In a news conference of November 30, 1950, Truman, peppered by questions from reporters, stated in unguarded fashion that the use of atomic weapons in Korea was an option always under consideration. His remarks were immediately reported by the United Press and the Associated Press and caused shock waves and fears of a wider war, across America and around the world, especially since the Soviet Union had acquired its own atomic bomb in 1949. (McCullough, *Truman*, 820-22.)

Bay St. Louis
Feb. 15, 1951 [misdated 1950]

My dear Arlette,

So many things have kept me from writing to you during the past two months, but you and your family have been in our thoughts almost constantly. All of us were <u>shocked</u> <u>beyond</u> <u>words</u> to read in your last letter what Maurice and Huguette had [. . . decided to do.] [The matter to which Emily refers was the decision of Maurice and Huguette to leave France and move, with their infant daughter Dorothée, to Argentina to live. (Edit.)] I know your mother and father are simply heartsick about it. And what a terrible shame that Jojo, who has studied so very hard, has had to leave school! But it is a blessing that Jojo is such a fine, responsible boy, who may be able to transform the necessity to work [in the family lithography business] into a golden opportunity to begin a prosperous career earlier than his classmates can begin theirs. We have already begun to worry, though, that he will have to go into military service [. . .]. Just think! Lorraine is nearer to you now, in distance, than your own darling little Dorothée. Well, you and Jojo will have to provide <u>other</u> *babies for Mme and M. Delattre!* That is the only solution.

I have reread your letter several times since I received it, especially the part about Maurice and the part about [. . . J. ——]. I have been thinking I might hear from you with further news almost any day, about the latter. Did he have anything definite to say at Christmas? Somehow, it annoys me to think of a girl as lovely and desirable as you are having to wait patiently until some <u>mere</u> <u>man</u> finds time to put into words the proposal he hints about! <u>Doggonit</u>, Arlette, that's just not the way it ought to be! I wonder whether you'd be happy with a man as busy as he is. Would he have enough time for his wife, if he is so enamored of his furs? At any rate, I'm just "on pins and needles," as our old saying goes, to hear more from you on this subject![57]

Since I haven't written you since Christmas, I do want to tell you that we had a delightful holiday, with Mother and Harry here with us for five days. I'm

---

[57] Arlette's interest in J. —— waned, and an engagement did not materialize.

enclosing some pictures we took on Christmas Eve and on Christmas morning, with two others I'd been saving for you since October. Also a clipping from the *Echo*. I think the colored pictures are especially good, don't you? René and I had a wonderful time on Christmas Eve, being Santa Claus for the first time! Of course, on both Lorraine's first and second Christmases, we gave her toys we told her Santa Claus brought, but she was too young to understand what we meant. This year, however, she had talked about Santa Claus ever since September! She knew all about him, sang songs about him all day, and talked about almost nothing else for weeks before Christmas arrived. On Christmas Eve she hung her stocking, and beside the Christmas tree she put a bottle of Coca Cola, a bottle opener, and a plate of cookies for Santa Claus. When she was asleep, René and I put all her new toys around the tree, drank the Coke, and ate the cookies, leaving the empty bottle and a few crumbs to add a realistic touch! René even wrote a note to her from Santa Claus, thanking her for his refreshments! The next morning she was so delighted and so happy over everything that we knew for the first time the joy of parenthood at Christmas time. Her red tricycle is her favorite plaything now. We are still having winter weather so that she can't go outdoors very much, but she rides the tricycle inside the house at top speed! You should see her! [. . .]

Poor René! He is so busy, now more than ever. Lorraine takes so much of my time now, and his mother and father hardly ever go to the store any more. He is at least 90% of the time alone, and that means he is doing the work of at least three people. We have tried employing people several times during the past few years, but every time the employee has been inefficient or has moved out of town after a few months. But René will have to have help this summer! He can't do everything alone when tourists begin arriving [. . .].

[Emily discusses her dissatisfaction with a professional photographer's photo of Lorraine, which she had hoped to send to M. Delattre for the final portrait of the family group.]

Here, we are all well and having our usual good times in spite of being so busy all the time. René and I went to a very gay New Year's Eve party at the Yacht Club and to a Carnival ball there last week. The Yacht Club has added so much to our little town. When you come back again, I know you'll enjoy it. We are going there tonight to a turkey supper about 8:30, when René closes the drugstore.

What do you think of the current world situation as compared with same about three months ago? In my humble opinion, it seems definitely more encouraging.[58] Incidentally, your M. René Pléven surely made a hit in Washington![59] All the reporters liked him tremendously, and his talks with various officials did a great deal to strengthen confidence in France's position in the world-picture today. By the way, one reporter said that M. Pléven one night went to visit an old friend in Washington and answered the telephone while he was there. It was a little girl calling to speak to the little girl who lived in the house. When M. Pléven answered the 'phone, he said, "This is the butler. Whom did you wish to speak to, mademoiselle?" The child was dumbfounded to think that her little friend's family had acquired a butler, but she has since been informed that she had the honor to speak, very unofficially, to the great prime minister of France! Probably she will always remember that she shared a joke with him when he was on a mission of international urgency![60] I am glad that we

---

[58] By February 1951 Matthew Ridgway and the U.S. Eighth Army had regained the initiative in Korea, progressively pushing back or killing large numbers of enemy troops and retaking lost territory. It was in the context of those most recent events that Emily allowed herself to feel that "the current world situation [...] seems definitely more encouraging."

[59] René Pléven, a moderate Socialist, was the eighth premier of the Fourth Republic, in office from July 1950 until the end of February 1951 (two weeks after the date of Emily's letter). He would return to power as the tenth premier from August 1951 until January 1952 and then would hold cabinet rank as Minister of Defense, serving until discredited by the French debacle at Dien Bien Phu in 1954.

[60] The "mission of international urgency" to which Emily refers was the beginning of discussions of the so-called Pléven Plan to integrate French and German army units into a European Defense Community, a scheme Pléven was advocating as an alternative to proposals by the United States, Great Britain, and Germany to reconstitute a separate German army. Pléven envisioned his proposal as the military companion-piece to Jean Monnet's and Robert Schuman's efforts to integrate French and German coal and steel production, efforts that would pave the way for the eventual emergence of the European Common Market. The Pléven Plan, which enjoyed at best only tepid support in France, would finally collapse under the joint assaults of the Gaullists and the political Left.

have men like your M. Pléven and our General Eisenhower in the world today,[61] aren't you?

Do you know, Arlette, René has dreamed <u>twice</u> during the last week that we were arriving in Paris and had just met you and your mother! He says he could see you both so vividly and the Arch of Triumph and the Eiffel Tower, too, and could even feel the suitcases in his hands! My, how I wish his dreams would come true!

Mr. de M. has just told me to tell you that we all miss you and wish so much you could come back. *And that's right!* And Mrs. de M. wants to know whether there are certain *denrées* [foodstuffs] Mme Delattre might be finding to be scarce in France now. If so, please let us know. Here nothing is scarce, but everything has advanced unreasonably in price. Our government is taking stringent measures now to curb inflation.[62] René is sure, however, that the Coast is soon to have an era of unusual prosperity, because a tremendous new aluminum plant is to be built immediately in New Orleans, a new 4-lane concrete bridge is to be built across the Bay, and both military bases at Gulfport and Biloxi will be vastly expanded. All this will give employment to thousands and bring new payrolls to our section.

We have just recovered from what one of the newspapers called the worst cold weather the Coast has had in 50 years. Even in Florida there was <u>snow</u>, and here the temperature was 17 degrees Fahrenheit—almost unheard-of cold for Bay St. Louis. Most of the lovely flowers were killed, all vegetable gardens destroyed, and almost every home had broken water pipes!

We shall all be waiting for your next letter; so write soon. Give our love to your parents and to Jojo.

---

[61] Eisenhower had been appointed Supreme Allied Commander, Europe, by Truman in December 1950.

[62] Freed of government price controls in the autumn of 1946, consumer prices had risen 19.5% by the end of 1946 and another 9.1% during the course of 1947. The years 1948-49 had brought a leveling-off of inflation (+3% in 1948; -2.4% in 1949), but in 1950 consumer prices had risen 5.3%. Despite the fact that the Truman Administration had imposed a wage-and-price freeze on January 26, 1951, consumer prices would rise an additional 6.8% during the course of the year. (Heller, ed., *Economics and the Truman Administration*, xvi.)

A big hug to you,
Emily

[From René]
P.S. My dear Arlette, many, many thanks for your beautiful Xmas gift. I'm enjoying it so much, and it is so unique. We certainly miss you, darling Arlette. Wish you could come see us again. All my love to all the family,
René

* * * * *

Bay St. Louis
March 19, 1951

My dear Arlette,

I am glad to have time to write you again, but really it is not such a happy occasion, after all. You see, the reason that I have some leisure time for writing is that I am sick in bed with the <u>mumps</u>! This is my third day in bed, and apparently I am destined not to have a very severe case. My face is not very swollen and there isn't much pain, either. My chief concern is that I feel sure Lorraine will soon develop the disease, too, because she has been thoroughly exposed to it by now. I know mumps is considered to be a childhood disease, but somehow as a child I escaped all the usual illnesses. I don't know how I happened to catch this case of mumps, unless I caught it at the movies. Many people in town have had it recently, but most of the patients are <u>children</u>!

Anyhow, it makes me feel quite undignified and very ridiculous! [. . .]

We were all so happy to have your last letter. Isn't it an incredible coincidence how you and I seem almost <u>always</u> to write each other at the same time, so that our letters cross each other over the Atlantic? I wouldn't be surprised if you were writing to me now. It must be about 10:30 at night in Paris as I write this. But, returning to your letter, it really was good to hear from you, even though you told us several disturbing things, your father's 'flu, for one thing. We have thought of him so often and we hope he is completely well again and that none of the rest of the family has had 'flu. We were disturbed, too, by what you wrote us about Maurice. I hate to think of Dorothée's having been so sick, and I <u>don't</u> <u>like</u> his suggestion that all of you go to Argentina! I think M. Delattre is right—it would be too hard to start all over again in a new part of the world! Don't you feel now as if the world is a little more secure than it was two or three months ago?[63] We do, and we would hate to see you leave your France! If you do, at any time in the future, I hope it will be <u>America</u> that you come to! Argentina is so pitifully under the dictatorship of Perón and his Evita that I cannot believe freedom-loving French people could find happiness there. Imagine—now even *La Prensa*, the largest Spanish newspaper in the world, has been suppressed because it dared to criticize Dictator Perón![64] You may have turmoil in France these days,[65] but at least you have freedom of speech and freedom of the press— and no dictatorship! No, if our opinion should be sought, we would all veto Mr. Maurice's plan (or should I say "<u>plot</u>"?).

It is good to know that Jojo is doing so well. What a joy he must be to all of you! I wish we could know him! He deserves a great deal of admiration.

But, Arlette, I really <u>don't</u> <u>know</u> what to think of that famous furrier of yours!!?! He should have said, "No! Never leave me to go to distant Argentina! <u>Marry</u> <u>me</u> <u>tonight</u>!" He is surely a most <u>unconventional</u> suitor! Sometimes I get angry and sometimes I have to laugh when I think about how he acts! [. . .] Maybe he's what we call in America "just not the marrying kind." [. . .]

---

[63] In Korea, Matthew Ridgway's Eighth Army was continuing to make gains and on March 15, four days before this letter, had recaptured Seoul.

[64] Emily's loathing for Juan Perón was fueled by the substantial coverage presented in *Time*, her favorite news magazine, of the suppression of *La Prensa* over the several weeks before she wrote this letter: "Argentina: Dirty Work," *Time*, February 5, 1951, p. 32; "The Press: *La Prensa* at War," ibid., February 12, 1951, pp. 45-46; and "Argentina: Murder at *La Prensa*, ibid., March 12, 1951, pp. 38-41.

[65] Three weeks earlier, René Pléven had resigned as premier, and, after protracted discussions, the Radical Henri Queuille had taken his place as tenth premier of the Fourth Republic. At the time that Emily wrote her letter, France was in the midst of a bruising debate over a new election law, which was designed to limit the power of the Gaullists and the Communists alike; Charles de Gaulle's opposition RPF was gaining strength; a price-rise was looming; the authoritarian Naegelen, governor-general of French Algeria, had just resigned; fighting was continuing in Indochina; and Paris was in the midst of a public transport strike.

Life here goes along much as usual, with plenty to do always. The Little Theater will soon present as its first play of the new year *Born Yesterday*, which has been very successful on Broadway and as a movie. Maybe we're too ambitious in the plays we select, but it's more fun to do the really good ones!

Be sure to see the movie called *All About Eve* if it comes to Paris. It's winning all sorts of awards for Bette Davis and Anne Baxter, and is one I know you'd enjoy.

Everyone sends much love to all the Delattres. (Funny, isn't it, how the s is added in English and not in French?) Write soon. Your letters are real treats for us all! Did you receive my letter with the Kodachrome pictures? I hope you liked them.

A big hug for you,
Emily

* * * * *

Bay St. Louis
July 26, 1951

Arlette chérie,

It seems impossible that I could sincerely want to write to you and yet see weeks pass by without finding a good time to do so! We need more than 24 hours in each day, I think!

I do hope the swimming suit reached you quickly and was satisfactory to you. I tried my best to find a two-piece Catalina suit for you, but I couldn't. You see, the summer you were here was the last year that two-piece suits were popular in America. By the next summer, styles had swung back toward one-piece suits––and this summer there are almost no two-piece suits on the beaches at all. The Jantzen suit I sent you was supposed to be a $15.00 suit (about the same price as Catalina suits), but it was on sale at $10.95. I thought it was very pretty, and I do so hope you like it too. The cap was a present to you from René. I sent the package by air as you suggested, because that way it would take only three days. It should have reached you about June 14. I am enclosing the sales slip.

Incidentally, you still have some money left in your American bank account—all of $1.68!!!

I'm enclosing also three pictures we took on Lorraine's 3rd birthday [. . .]. She's growing up so fast and using such grown-up words now—like "satisfied," "repair," "comfortable," etc. [. . .]. She's getting a social-responsibility sense, too, because she thinks often about the "poor little children in Korea" and wishes she could give them some of her food or her clothes. I wish so very much you could come back to visit us again, because Lorraine would be a real joy to you now [. . .]

All of us read and reread your last long, wonderful letter! Of course we were especially interested in the part about your furrier [. . .]. To tell you the truth, none of us has a high regard for J. —— any longer. And again I say, as in my last letter, we don't think you've found "honest-to-goodness" real love yet [. . .]. I can understand how many things besides love must be considered in a marriage, but marriage without love would be a terrible situation, in my opinion. And I don't believe you are in love at all. Are you really?

I hope that you have not decided to go to England. Somehow I think that that would be a mistake. You have built a reputation for yourself in Paris, and I think you should stay there. I want you to marry a Frenchman, too, and live near your family so you can all always see each other often! You see, we have planned your life for you, "little sister"! [. . .]

I've given two parties during the last month—one a 4-table bridge party and one a luncheon. Both were at the Yacht Club. I wish you could have been here to go with me [. . .].

During the celebrations for the birthday of Paris[66] we listened to several radio broadcasts describing the festivities and saw a wonderful newsreel about it. What a city of marvels Paris must be! We dream constantly of the day when we shall leave to visit you there! [. . .]

---

[66] This appears to be a reference to the 1500th anniversary of the turning away of Attila and his Huns from their planned attack upon Paris in A.D. 451 after the prayers of Ste Geneviève for heavenly intervention.

Write us soon, and give your family our love. We hope you are all well. It is tragic that you cannot see Dorothée as she grows up.

Lots of love from us all,
Emily

P.S. Don't even <u>think</u> of going to Argentina!! Perón is getting to be a small-scale Hitler. Incidentally, <u>I</u> believe Hitler is right there in Argentina today with other henchmen of his!

* * * * *

Bay St. Louis, Miss.
October 1, 1951

Dear Madame Delattre, Arlette, and Jojo,

    No letter can possibly express the sorrow of our entire family over your terrible loss.[67] Your cablegram was such a shock to us that we still can hardly realize its sad news is true. We know how much M. Delattre meant to his family and what a loving husband and father he must have been, and our hearts ache for you. <u>I</u> feel particular sympathy for Arlette and Jojo, because I lost my father several years ago, and I can understand so well how they feel now. But like me too, they have happy, proud memories of him and a wonderful mother to whom to turn, and both receive and give comfort.

    It's a strange thing, but on the very day M. Delattre died, René and I were looking at the portraits and the other three pictures he painted, and I had said that in my next letter to Arlette I wanted to tell him once again how much we love his gifts. The landscape of the viaduct and the river near Le Perreux in particular has the most <u>soothing</u>, <u>restful</u> effect on me. Never a day passes that I do not stop to look at it and <u>feel</u> some of the peacefulness of it.

    When you feel like writing, Arlette, please do. We shall be anxious to hear from you. I hope you received our cablegram. We have all thought of all of

---

[67] Georges Delattre, Sr., died from a sudden and unexpected heart attack in late September 1951.

you so much during these last few days, which must have been such difficult ones for you.

    I have told most of your friends about your cablegram, and everyone is so sorry and sympathetic. Mrs. Sporl asked me to convey her sympathy, and so did [. . . Venie's sisters]. Several of your friends asked for your address so that they might write you themselves.

    I shall write again soon. I want to tell you about our new home that we are building at last.

    Mr. and Mrs. de Montluzin and René join me in giving all of you once again our deepest sympathy. Please extend our sympathy also to Maurice and to M. René Delattre. We are awaiting a letter from you.

Much love always,
Emily

* * * * *

Bay St. Louis
October 17, 1951

Dearest Arlette,

    Your letter written three days ago reached us tonight, and oh, how our hearts ache for all of you! We have thought of you constantly ever since the cablegram came, but all the details in your letter have made even more vivid the terrible loss you have suffered. It must have been very painful for you to write that letter to us, and we are grateful for your courage. We agree that it was a blessing that your adored father did not suffer. We always had that consolation in thinking of <u>my</u> father's death, too—and though the shock is a terrible one for your family and you, it is so much better this way than to see your loved one suffer for weeks and die slowly, as so many do. However, all the brave <u>words</u> in the world cannot fill the emptiness in your home, I know—but <u>time</u> is a wonderful healer, and you have the great joy of remembering only goodness and happiness and love in connection with M. Delattre. He must have been so much like my own "Daddy." I have never been able to recall a single moment of his life when he was not just the wonderful, gentle, truly good father you have described in your letter. Do you know what his idea was about immortality—or "life after death"? He felt that in a way he would continue to live in the lives of those his life had affected. He taught Harry and me to be honest, for example—and when we choose honesty as our course, he is living in us again. M. Delattre still lives in the calmness and strength of Jojo, in the loving loyalty you show your mother, in the beauty he captured in his paintings, in oh, so many ways! I am probably expressing my thoughts poorly, but perhaps you can understand what I mean.

We are wondering if you received our cablegram, which we sent the same morning yours arrived. If you think of it when you write again, please let us know. We hope it reached you. We love you all so much and wish the ocean did not separate us.

In the matter of your future plans, we agree unanimously with your belief that you should keep the *printing business* and continue to operate it! We should all be distressed to learn that you had sold it and gone to Argentina. It (*the printing business*) is security for all of you, and if it were converted into a sum of money, that money might soon take wings and be gone! At any rate, if you should leave France (which we do not think you should do!) for goodness' sake don't go to a dictator-ridden land like Argentina! There you have only Maurice and his child to love you, and the country is certain to have a disturbed, unhappy future, as all dictatorships do. In America you would have many relatives and friends to love and help you—and you would not lose the freedom so dear to Frenchmen everywhere.

But we all feel that you, with the help of your mother, Jojo, and M. René, can make a real success of operating your business. You will feel more self-confidence every day, and you are intelligent and capable, Arlette! Think of all the women who have made business successes! You can, too, even if everything is gloomy and confusing at the moment. Don't be discouraged, and don't make any decisions too quickly.

I do want to tell you briefly about our house. We are building it at last, on our lot across the street, you remember. It will be finished before Christmas, and we think it will be beautiful. This is a rough sketch of the floor plan: [. . .]. [Here

Emily includes a careful, hand-drawn sketch showing in detail the layout of the ranch-style, three-bedroom home.]

As you can see, there are many windows, some of them corner windows. All the rooms are large, and there are lots of closets. The kitchen will have all the wonderful modern appliances, including a dishwasher and even a machine for <u>drying</u> clothes!

In my next letter I'll tell you more about it, but for now I think this is enough. I would not have mentioned it at all, except that I thought it might please you to know that we are soon to have a lovely home of our own.

I know how occupied you will be, but I hope that you will have time to write us even <u>one</u> <u>page</u> occasionally to let us know what is happening. We shall be so anxious to know your decisions. I am so sorry you had to leave Marie Christiane, but I understand that there was no other choice to make.

Please give your mother and Jojo a kiss from us. We will all write often, and we hope you know that you are always in our thoughts. And we <u>know</u> that somehow you three will find strength and wisdom to carry on.

We embrace all of you,
Emily

* * * * *

Bay St. Louis
January 15, 1952

My dear Arlette,

In a few days we shall hang our portraits and our beautiful river scene on the walls of our new home, and so, when you and your dear mother and Georges visit us some day, you will see something of your Papa's genius over here in America, adding so much beauty to our home.

But before I begin to describe our wonderful house to you, let me tell you that your package reached us in excellent condition a week after Christmas and that we are all delighted over our gifts and very touched to think that you took the time and trouble to send them to us at a time when your hearts are so heavy.

Knowing the conditions under which you shopped for them and mailed them, we value them more than ever. I love my pin—it's beautiful! (In fact, the night of the day I received it, I went with René and my mother and Harry to a party at Ada Whitfield's—and I wore three Christmas gifts of yours!—the pin, the black suede bag, and the *Coeur-Joie*! And René wore his beautiful grey suede belt, so we were all decked out in finery from France. Mrs. de Montluzin is so pleased with her perfume, and so is Mr. de M. with his book. He took a one-day trip to Fontainebleau while he was in France as a boy, and your book has refreshed his memory of it. All of us are enchanted with Lorraine's gift. That soft, soft pink leather is lovely, and the suitcase shape is so original. I think you have spoiled us with such lovely presents, and we all thank all of you very, very much.

We were so glad to receive your long letter, as well as your New Year note and Georges's. We think of all of you every day that passes, and when a letter from you comes, we are like people hungry for news. We know that it must have been a hard decision to make about selling the factory [i.e., the lithography business], but undoubtedly it was the wisest one. Will you go back to your former work when it is sold? I hope so, since you enjoyed it so much. René was saying yesterday that if you should come to America, you could so easily find good employment in New Orleans with your experience in Paris and your ability to speak three languages. I do so hope you will all decide to come to America if you leave France. At any rate, while Georges is in military service, you can consider the whole problem at your leisure and come to a good decision.

Speaking of that, when will he have to enter the service? And is there much talk in France about General Eisenhower's decision of last week?[68] René and I feel that, although he would be a wonderful president, he should stay in his present position.[69] What do you think?

And now I must tell you something about our new home! It is almost finished, and we plan to move into it about the first of February. It's really beautiful, Arlette, and I can't wait for you to see it [. . .]. [Emily describes the

---

[68] Eisenhower on January 7, 1952, had announced in Paris his willingness to accept the nomination of the Republican Party for president.
[69] As NATO commander

colors of each room and ends with a glowing tribute to the kitchen:] The kitchen is really the best room of all, in a way. Just let me tell you what we have in it! A Westinghouse electric stove with all sorts of amazing features to make cooking easy and pleasant; a big, double Youngstown sink with double drain board; a Youngstown electric <u>dishwasher</u> (Isn't that heavenly?); a Westinghouse refrigerator that defrosts itself automatically—in fact, it does so continuously so that frost never seems to form at all!; a Westinghouse washing machine (the best one of all leading brands, we think); and best of all, a Westinghouse <u>clothes</u> <u>dryer</u>! Just think, no clothes to hang out on a line or bring in wet if a rain should come! Oh, yes, and there's an electric hot water heater that is like a white porcelain tabletop cabinet. I think I can find pictures of most of these marvels, and if I can, I'll enclose them. This is a sketch of the kitchen: [. . .]. [A drawing of the U-shaped arrangement of the kitchen and the appliances follows.]

We have had to buy most of our furniture, though Mrs. de M. has given us a handsome mirror, a marble-topped table, and several antique pieces which were up in the attic and which we have had reupholstered or refinished. Also, she had given Lorraine about two years ago a rosewood bed and the big rosewood dresser in our bedroom (Remember it?); so we will use those to furnish our guest room until Lorraine is old enough to use them herself [. . .]. [Emily gives further descriptions of the built-in furniture and numerous cabinets and storage areas.]

I could write about our house forever, but I'll stop. Just one thing more, though— Since I'll soon be cooking, I'd love to have two or three of your favorite recipes. Won't you and Mme Delattre decide on a few and send them to me?

I wish you could hear Lorraine singing the *Marseillaise* at the top of her voice these days. She sings all day long, many songs, but the *Marseillaise* is one of her best-loved ones. You should have seen her on the Sunday before Christmas: The children of the Episcopal church gave a program about Christmas at the morning church service, and as a special surprise Lorraine sang the carol *It Came upon the Midnight Clear* all by herself [. . .].

We were all happy to get the picture of Dorothée. She's <u>adorable</u>, Arlette, so dainty and doll-like. If only you could see her often! (But don't go to

Argentina to do it!!!!) I'm so afraid that when Maurice comes next month, you will let him talk you into doing just that. And <u>especially</u> <u>for</u> <u>your</u> <u>mother</u> I think that would be a tragic mistake. Do you think she would like to work in New Orleans too? I feel quite sure she <u>could</u>.

  We thought of you often on your birthday. We had had a big New Year's Eve before it, but we didn't forget you. Several people gave parties on New Year's Eve—open-house affairs, where one stayed only a short time, so we went to four of them that evening! One was at Dr. Samuel's—they always ask about you—and the last one, where we welcomed the New Year in with champagne, was at Dot and Dan Russell's [. . .].

  By the way, we have a wide new sand beach now, pumped in by the new bridge constructors. It stretches from Effie McCulloch's home almost to ours and will be very pleasant this summer.

  René and his mother and father ask me to send their love to you, Mme Delattre, and Georges. And you know I always send mine! Write us again when you can. I hope our package reached you.

                Much love,
                Emily

     * * * * *

                Bay St. Louis
                May 17, 1952

My dear Arlette,

  The month of May will always be <u>your</u> <u>month</u> to us, and we have been missing you more than ever, especially during the last week. When you look at the enclosed pictures of Lorraine, you will realize very vividly how long you've been away. Just think—she was only two months old when you came! How we wish you could come back and bring your mother and Jojo with you! But in a way, you've never left us <u>really</u>, because not only the ones in our family but also our friends speak of you and think about you so very often. It is a great compliment to you that you are evidently someone who cannot be forgotten, even by casual acquaintances [. . .].

Before I write anything about us, I must tell you how very glad we all are that you and Mme Delattre and Georges decided not to sell your father's business! We feel that you were very wise to keep it, and we are so proud of all three of you for working so hard and determinedly to make it a success! It is hard to say which one of you we feel most proud of—maybe Georges for accepting so suddenly and so capably a man's responsibilities, both in business and at home—maybe Mme Delattre, for putting aside her grief enough to leave her home each day and reenter the business in order to do all she can for it—and maybe you, Arlette dear, for giving up, without a word of complaint, the place you had just made for yourself in the world of fashion! We realize how much it has hurt you, not only to lose your beloved father but at the same time to sacrifice all you had worked for in your position at Marie Christiane's. We do admire and respect all of you so much, and we know that when such courage as you have shown is involved, the business cannot help but become a huge success. I am sure your father would applaud what you are doing [. . .]. [Emily expresses her delight that the family has decided not to be influenced by Maurice's urgings to move to Argentina.] And we think the plan to take the designer into the business with you was an excellent one, a very astute idea. You don't know how interested we are in all of this—we have discussed it over and over, and are anxious for your next letter. I hope things are smoother now. How wonderful about Georges's military deferment!

Thank you for the snapshots. We were delighted to receive them. Those of you and Jojo on vacation looked like movie stars! And the recent ones in the office were very impressive. You look so pretty and so efficient that I should think clients would be happy to do business with you! And Georges looks just as capable and handsome himself. I hope you'll send more pictures soon.

Speaking of pictures, I don't know why I haven't yet taken any of the house or any indoor pictures either. I will, though, and will send some in my next letter. I want you all to see how M. Delattre's paintings look in our new home. We are so very happy here and never have stopped looking about us and exclaiming "Isn't it beautiful?" Every week or so we acquire something new, and each addition is something to rejoice about. For instance, last week Mrs. Sporl made us a present of a lovely floor-lamp, and on Mother's Day Mrs. de Montluzin gave me a beautiful yellow bedspread which carries out the color of our bedroom perfectly. Father's Day is next month, but I have already presented René with his gift so that he might be enjoying it now—a chaise longue for the screened porch! I know that some day you will see our lovely home, but I do so wish you could come now while everything is shiny-new. Well, we'll try to keep it all that way for you, anyhow!

Speaking of Mrs. Sporl, I do want to tell you something she said. I know you will be surprised, so prepare for a shock! We saw her last week—we took Lorraine to Audubon Park and Pontchartrain Beach [in New Orleans]—and when I told her that you often inquire about her in your letters, she said, "You know, I love Arlette. In fact, when she was here, my hope was that she and Junior would fall in love and marry. Nothing would have made me happier!" Now, what do you think of that? You really made an impression on her, didn't you? [. . .]

Bay St. Louis has a fine new beach at last! When the construction company which is building the new bridge had to pump out a lot of sand at the entrance to the bridge, the sand was pumped in from a point past your little beach in front of the hotel on down past the Episcopal church. It formed a wide, lovely beach, and the city has placed playground equipment there for the children and built good steps going down there [. . .].

We are all well and busy as ever—in fact, busier! René has a new clerk at the drugstore—an inexperienced young girl, but one who is learning well and is willing to work. I know she will save him many steps this summer. You should see how slim he is! He really looks good. And I keep busy as a bee with my housework and Lorraine. I am getting along quite well with my cooking, and I'm looking forward to the recipes you'll send. (A cookbook, as you suggested, would be wonderful some time, too!)

There are, as usual, lots of parties going on. Jane Blair and Alicia Rollins both married on Mardi Gras weekend, and many people entertained in their honor. I did, among others. It was our first party in our new house, and René laughed and said, "Remember, the party is for Jane and Alicia. You act as if it's the debut of the house!" (And it really was!)

René and I are planning on attending one day and night of a state pharmaceutical convention to be held next month in Biloxi. They are always lots of fun and very good for making new friendships and renewing old ones.

I hate to think about world affairs these days, don't you? What a terrible situation the world is in!! In our <u>national</u> affairs, René and I hope our next president will be General Eisenhower.[70]

Mr. and Mrs. de Montluzin send all of you their love [. . .]. Write us <u>soon</u>. And have courage!

I embrace you,
Emily

* * * * *

Bay St. Louis
July 23, 1952

Arlette dear,

We were so delighted to get your long letter and to find pictures enclosed in it. All of you look charming and all of you show that indefinable French air which the rest of the world can recognize but cannot copy. I believe I would know at a glance that you three people were French! I am enclosing pictures I've been saving for you for two months. I'm sorry they are not in color, because the soft, clear pastel colors inside our home are a large part of its beauty. The outside is painted white, with a dark green trim around the window screens—and now at last, after four months of almost unceasing work, we have a smooth green lawn!

---

[70] At the time that Emily was writing, the stalemate was continuing in Korea, with the three-month-long Battle of Hill Eerie then in progress; and the vituperative 1952 presidential election campaign was well underway. By this time Emily and René clearly had set aside the reservations Emily had expressed in her letter of January 15, 1952, concerning Eisenhower's presidential aspirations.

You see, the yard was filled in with many truckloads of red clay, which was leveled by a tractor. There was not one piece of grass to be seen when the tractor finished about the first of April. We planted grass seed and have almost constantly watered the young grass to keep it alive during this hot, dry summer. Now we can look with pride, though, on a lovely green lawn all around our white house. With the eight big pecan trees, which form a ring around the yard, and the thick green grass, the house has a very pleasant setting. So far, our only blooming flowers are zinnias, but we have about ten small hydrangea bushes[71] growing well and six azaleas, too. This fall we shall plant other things. René gets up about six o'clock in the morning once or twice a week and cuts grass both here and at his mother's and father's home. He says he really enjoys it at that hour, and with the power-mower he can keep both yards looking lovely.

    I am sorry I have no pictures of myself to send you. Usually, I am alone with Lorraine when I take pictures. But next time I'll try to send some of me, too.

    We were very happy to know that your business is progressing well and that you are doing work again for such a big movie company as United Artists. We feel that your decision was right—not to admit into partnership a man about whom you felt any doubts or hesitation. Surely your hardest time is behind you now—all the shock, the reorganization, the learning of primary facts of running the business. From now on I believe things will be easier and smoother—and maybe some day even Maurice will admit that you did right and that he is proud of you! Over here, we are very proud of all of you!

    Speaking of pride, we felt quite proud of Mr. de Montluzin recently, too. René and I attended one day's session at the State Pharmaceutical Convention in Biloxi, as I told you we would, and went to the banquet and ball that night. (Incidentally, we had a wonderful time!) During the evening one of the State officials asked René to try to get his father to drive over the next day, because it had been decided to place his name before the Convention as a nominee for the Honorary President of the State Association for the coming year. (He is now 86,

---

[71] All ten hydrangeas were given to Emily and René by Venie's maid, Margaret Favre, who had made cuttings from her own plants.

you know, and the oldest active pharmacist in the State of Mississippi!) So, with a little persuasion and encouragement, Papa[72] agreed to go, and the next day the drugstore was closed for six hours while all of us, even Lorraine, went to Biloxi to see him get his honorary presidency! He was asked to come up and speak over the microphone, but he was emotionally upset and could say only "Thank you!" He was presented with a trophy, and quite a few pictures were taken of him. You will see an article about him in one of the June issues of the *Echo*.

We were distressed to learn of the long illness and death of your Uncle René's wife. Please convey to him our deep sympathy. Have you read of the new treatment of cancer by "cobalt bomb" rays? So far, there are only two hospitals (both in Canada) equipped for such treatment, but soon there will be seven more (five in the U.S.). The cures have been so spectacular that it is hoped that cancer is finally being conquered. The "cobalt bomb" is somehow a product of atomic energy and is exposed to uranium to absorb certain potent rays. Maybe soon cancer will have lost its dreadfulness.

You asked about Mrs. Sporl's statement. She has made it again, both to René and me, when she called us on the telephone on July 14th [Bastille Day] to wish us all a happy day. (You see, we do not forget July 14th even over here! Lorraine telephoned Papa that morning and sang the *Marseillaise* for him.) Mrs. Sporl had just received your letter, and again she said, "I do so wish Arlette and Junior had married!" But I do not know whether she has ever mentioned such a thing to Junior or not! [. . .]

I know you must have greatly enjoyed the automobile show, and you must have looked lovely in such beautiful clothes. I haven't seen the last *Geographic* yet, but I shall look for Papa's copy of it right away.

I hope you will all enjoy your vacation more than ever this year, because you have worked so hard and so well deserve some fun and relaxation. We shall be thinking of you. Mother and Harry will arrive here on August 10th for a two weeks' trip. They have not seen our home since Christmas, when it was still uncompleted.

---

[72] Pronounced with the accent firmly on the second syllable in this Franco-American family

Please give our love to Mme Delattre and to Jojo. Have a good time next month, and write when you get home. I shall be thinking carefully, as you suggested, about something from France for *our house*.

Much, much love from us all,
Emily

P.S. We saw in a newsreel the celebrations in honor of Louis Braille. Also a television play about his life.

P.P.S. We are delighted that Eisenhower received the Republican nomination. We are following both conventions on radio and television[73] and find them fascinating entertainment as well as serious politics!

* * * * *

Bay Saint Louis
December 9, 1952

Dearest Arlette,

I wish you knew how eager we are to hear from you! Your last letter was months ago, and we have been waiting for another for a long time now! Did you receive my letter containing all the snapshots of Lorraine and of our house?

We were delighted with your two pictures, which arrived after I had written to you. They have given us a great deal of pleasure, and we've shown them with pride to many of your friends. All of us are so proud to think that you won the prize when you were the only girl who was not a movie star or a professional model! You looked lovely and radiant—and your clothes and the car were beautiful. Thank you so much for sending the picture to us.

When I mail this card and note tomorrow, I shall also send by air mail a small package of gifts for you all. I hope they will reach you in time for Christmas Day. They will bring with them much love from all of us.

---

[73] The 1952 presidential election campaign was only the second in which American voters could watch a national nominating convention on television.

This will be our first Christmas in our new home, so it will have a special significance for us. Besides, Lorraine is old enough now to enjoy helping with holiday decorations and gift-wrapping, etc. And she can hardly wait for Santa Claus. Can you believe it—most of the things she wants him to bring her are <u>cowboy</u> things! But my friends tell me that is typical of four-year-olds, whether boys or girls!

Mr. de M. celebrated his 87th birthday last week, and last month René and I celebrated our 10th wedding anniversary. To mark the occasion we had azaleas planted all across the front of our house. They will look lovely this spring.

Please give our wishes for a pleasant Christmas to your mother and Georges and remember us to your Uncle René. I know this will be a hard Christmas for him. And <u>please</u> <u>write</u> <u>soon</u>, Arlette.

Much love,
Emily

* * * * *

Bay St. Louis
February 22, 1953

My dear Arlette,

How happy we were when your two packages arrived, and how delighted with the thoughtfulness of your selections for us all! The watercolors are exquisite and the two we chose will add so much to our home. We are keeping the smaller pair and intend to have them framed very simply against a soft gray background, which will blend perfectly with the colors of our bedroom. Mr. and Mrs. de Montluzin are charmed by the larger pair and are planning to have them framed soon. Please extend our thanks also to your mother and Georges.

As for Lorraine's gift, you could not have made a happier choice. It arrived just a week before Mardi Gras, and I am sure you must have been picturing her in it on that day. It is a beautiful costume, and she looks like a little Dutch doll in it. I took some pictures of her as she watched the parade that day, and I am sure I shall have them back in tomorrow's mail so that I can put them in with the others in this letter. We did not go to New Orleans for Mardi Gras this year because the Bay St. Louis parade is quite thrilling for children, and many of Lorraine's little friends who are in school were to be on floats, and she wanted to see them, of course. It was cold that day, too. I was so sorry she had to wear a coat over her pretty costume. Everyone thought the felt appliqués on it were so unusual and lovely.

Speaking of the Carnival festivities, this season's Carnival Ball meant a great deal to us— Margaret Shadoin [Lorraine's godmother] was the Queen, and she chose as her four little train-bearers and attendants Lorraine, Dale Russell, Bobby Whitfield, and Linda McCulloch. (I know you remember Dot Russell, Ada Whitfield, and Effie McCulloch.) Everything was kept very secret until the final night of the ball—even the children did not tell a soul that they were participating in it! Except for singing at church twice, this was Lorraine's first real public appearance; René says she made her <u>debut</u> that night! She was so happy to be an attendant for Margaret and so thrilled over her beautiful dress that it never occurred to her to be nervous or timid. In fact, all four children were as poised and gracious and dignified as if they had taken part in pageants all their lives. The little girls' dresses were made with 2 circular white tulle skirts over two white taffeta skirts <u>over</u> three tarlatan skirts <u>over</u> an organdy hoop-skirt! The top tulle skirt had a wide panel of lace-edged ruffles at the back, and there were lace and tulle ruffles around the neck. I know you won't be able to believe this, Arlette, but there are <u>44</u> <u>yards</u> of material in Lorraine's dress!! It doesn't seem possible, does it? The skirts were very, very bouffant, and all three little girls looked adorable. They wore half-circles of tiny white flowers in their hair, like a coronet, and carried little old-fashioned bouquets of pink, blue, and white flowers. The little boy wore a miniature full-dress suit just like all the men. They followed the Queen out and walked behind her in all the various marching the King & Queen had to do. Then they stood beside her on the stage all during the pageant presented in her honor and during the time afterwards when everyone came up on the stage to greet their majesties. At last, when dancing began, René, who was one of the floor committeemen, came up on the stage and asked Lorraine to dance. She was just like Cinderella at the ball, she said, and René was like the Prince!

Afterwards, we took her to her Papa's home, and for the first time in her life she slept with him! René and Mrs. de M. and I went on to a champagne party for the king and queen at the Seals' home, and then to the Yacht Club for the supper-dance that always follows the Carnival Ball. I wish you could have seen how lovely Margaret looked. Her gown was of white nylon net with appliqués of lace and rhinestones. Her mantle was of dark red velvet edged with ermine, and she wore a rhinestone crown and carried red roses and a rhinestone scepter. The king was someone I'm sure you don't remember. René was very handsome in his full dress suit, and he received so many compliments from admiring ladies (!) that, with plenty of champagne besides, he had one of the most gala evenings of his life, I think! As for me, I wore an aqua net dress made over aqua taffeta, with a matching stole and rose-red carnations. (I didn't intend to write at such length about what happened on one evening, but it was all so much fun, especially seeing Lorraine's enjoyment, that I've not been able to stop describing it.)

On Wednesday of this week I'm giving a luncheon for Margaret. Most of your friends will be here. It is so good to be able to entertain in our own lovely home.

I have been very busy recently, meeting with the library board members about a gift which has been offered us. We have only a small town library, occupying two rooms in a public building several blocks away from the beach. Now an English lady [Ruth Knowles] who came here to live about six months ago has decided that she would like to give to Bay St. Louis her entire collection of books. There are over 7,000 volumes, valued at about $20,000.00! The books are an almost complete coverage of the best in English and American literature of all centuries, besides many French, Italian, German, Irish, and Scandinavian classics. There are poetry, fiction, travel, biography, drama, encyclopedias, dictionaries, and even phonograph records of poems and plays! Naturally, we cannot turn such an incredible offer down, and obviously to accept it we must have an entire building for the library, preferably one near the beach and the business section. Already several people have offered donations toward a new building. Mrs. Samuel, for instance, has offered a thousand dollars. But you can see what a complicated affair I am involved in, as president of the library board. I hope it will all work out well and that when I write again, I can tell you the project is well under way [. . .].

We have all been so shocked recently on reading about the Oradour trials.[74] I feel that European unity is an absolute necessity, which must be accomplished, but I cannot understand how French people could ever trust an armed German.[75] So much unspeakable crime for centuries could not be forgotten. Yet with a plan like the Schuman plan beginning to bear fruit, and with a man like M. Jean Monnet as a leader, perhaps some sort of basic unity may become a reality.[76]

We thought so often of all of you during the flu epidemic in France. We heard that in your country alone there were fifteen million cases of it! Surely hope none of you was ill. I am sure that by this time you have completely

---

[74] In one of the most notorious war crimes perpetrated in France, virtually the entire population of the village of Oradour-sur-Glane near Limoges was murdered on June 10, 1944, by a battalion of Waffen-SS troops, after the German military had received a tip that an SS officer was being held prisoner by the Resistance in another village, Oradour-sur-Vayres. Ordered to assemble in the square for identity checks, the local men were marched to barns and sheds and machine-gunned to death; the women and children were herded into the village church, where they were likewise murdered by machine-gun fire. The total death toll was 642, including 205 children. The empty village was then looted and partially destroyed.

Sixty-five survivors of the SS battalion were finally put on trial before a military tribunal in Bordeaux on January 12, 1953. All but 21 were tried in absentia, since East Germany refused extradition requests for the accused living within its borders. Of the 21 who were present for trial, 14 were Frenchmen from Alsace, including one who had willingly enlisted in the German army and 13 who had been conscripted at age 17 (against their will, according to their lawyers). On February 11, 20 of the 21 were convicted, prompting furious indignation in Alsace and demands for amnesty for the Alsatian conscripts. To the disgust of the Limousin region surrounding the remains of Oradour-sur-Glane, the Chamber of Deputies hastily bowed to the protests from Alsace and on February 19 (three days before Emily wrote her letter) granted amnesty to all of the French participants save the one willing enlistee, who was subsequently executed.

[75] Here Emily refers again to the Pléven Plan, brainchild of René Pléven, who was serving at that time as Minister of Defense in Premier René Mayer's ministry (the thirteenth of the Fourth Republic). The Pléven Plan to integrate units of the French and German armies into a European Defense Community, sapped by lukewarm support and strongly opposed by both extremes of the political spectrum, was stumbling toward collapse.

[76] A reference to Jean Monnet's and Robert Schuman's establishment of the European Coal and Steel Community, which successfully integrated French and German coal and steel production and thus laid the groundwork for the later emergence of the European Common Market.

recovered from your operation.[77] Probably it was the only way to make you take a good rest.

Our hearts have been very sad this week because of all the suffering and destruction caused by the terrible floods in Europe.[78] Our radios reported details day and night until we felt as if we were almost there ourselves.

Please tell your Uncle René that Papa was touched with emotion on receiving his letter and is now engaged in composing a reply to it. I am sure he will mail it soon.

Best love from all of us to all of you. Write soon.

I embrace you,
Emily

* * * * *

Bay St. Louis
September 22, 1953

My dear Arlette,

I don't like to think how long it has been since I last wrote to you. Please forgive me and make excuses for me! This has been the busiest summer we have ever had, not only in our business but also at home, since we have had numerous visitors and life has been quite full from day to day [. . .].

You can imagine our surprise and pleasure when we actually held your long-awaited journal[79] in our hands! We have read it with close attention and the deepest interest. You have a real talent for writing, Arlette, and a knack for observing details and selecting those that are significant. The section about Bay

---

[77] Emily's letters shed no further light on Arlette's operation, and Arlette's letter on the subject was destroyed by Hurricane Katrina.

[78] In early February 1953 catastrophic floods had struck The Netherlands, southeastern England, northern France, Belgium, and parts of Germany, causing hundreds of deaths and massive destruction of homes and farmland. The floods were most devastating in The Netherlands, where the dikes were breached in numerous places.

[79] Arlette's diary—her *journal*—which she had kept while on her visit to America in 1948 and to which she had added historical notes after her return to France

St. Louis and New Orleans brought back to us the vivid memories of many incidents we had completely forgotten, and we felt as if we were reliving those happy days again. Your descriptions of Washington and New York and your characterization of Mrs. Doll were especially well done, I think. To be entirely honest with you, I must admit that there were a few points, particularly in some of your generalizations about the behavior of Americans as a whole, on which we did not agree with you. But on the whole we felt that you showed remarkable powers of observation and journalistic skill, and we only wished the journal were longer! In fact, the last few pages were missing. Page 122 was the last one we received [. . .].

We have often remarked, and especially lately, that it is a pity your visit could not have been made a little later, because each year brings improvements you would have liked to Bay St. Louis. For example, the Yacht Club, the sand beach, the library (!), a municipal pier, three new schools, several very nice stores—and of course the beautiful new bridge. It was opened to traffic on August 1 and is a structure the national highway system can well be proud of. It's concrete and very wide, with plenty of room for six cars passing each other at one time. There's a sidewalk on each side, and at night the lights are like a necklace of diamonds thrown in a shining arc across the blackness of the Bay. The old wooden bridge is now being removed, a process which will require about two months more. If you were here now, no fire nor storm could prevent your "date" [from across the bay] from crossing the bridge to take you out! [. . .]

Our chief topic of conversation nowadays is what happens <u>at school</u>!—because Lorraine is now in kindergarten at one of the new schools I mentioned. She is delighted with it and tells us that "every day is better than a birthday party"! There are twenty children in her class, all 4- and 5-year-olds, and they have an excellent teacher. I take her to school at nine every morning and go to get her again at twelve. You can imagine how empty the house seems during those three hours! [. . .] [Emily describes a typical school day for the kindergarten class and mentions Lorraine's continued pleasure in drawing and a few of the new words such as "collapsible tables," "rectangular," and "amazed" that she comes home using.]

We have been reading a great many articles this summer about the war in Indochina and about the political and economic situation in France.[80] I do hope M. Laniel[81] will be successful in making his reforms and establishing a firm government. (By the way, Virginia Seal was on the Riviera during the big national strike. Wasn't that an ideal place to be detained?) We feel encouraged about the war just now. Don't you think the outlook is more hopeful there? General Navarre[82] seems to be a leader of much energy, and apparently he is now receiving real support [. . .]. [The remainder of the letter is missing.]

* * * * *

Bay St. Louis
December 13, 1953

My dear Arlette,

We were so happy to receive your long letter and to know that all of you are well and spent such a pleasant vacation last summer. After Christmas I'll write a real letter to tell you all the happenings here—but for now, this is just a note to say we'll be thinking of all of you at Christmas and hoping you have a very happy holiday. And when the New Year comes, we'll be sending "Happy Birthday" thoughts your way, with the wish that 1954 will bring you personal happiness and business prosperity.

We mailed a package to you about a week ago and hope it will arrive in time for Christmas. I must tell you that we are sending the same gift to each one

---

[80] In addition to the escalating war in Indochina, a number of economic problems confronted France in the summer and autumn of 1953: a budget deficit, a tax system that brought in insufficient tax receipts for the nation's needs, an unfavorable balance of trade, inflation, and high unemployment. In addition, the government was contending with *Poujadisme*, a populist tax revolt fueled by mass meetings and angry rhetoric, which pitted the lower middle class in the cities and countryside against the wealthy.

[81] Joseph Laniel, premier of the fourteenth of the twenty-one ministries of the Fourth Republic (June 26, 1953-June 12, 1954), had announced on August 4, 1953, a series of austerity measures that would especially affect public employees. The resultant general strike that began on August 7 would continue for two and a half weeks, bringing much of France to a standstill.

[82] Henri Eugène Navarre had assumed command of the French forces in Indochina in May 1953.

of you, because René, Lorraine, and I all have some of the same kind of things and we are so delighted with them that we thought all three of you would like some, too! (Don't I sound mysterious?) These gifts are very cozy and warm on cold evenings and early mornings! (And in case you wonder about this when you see them, they are completely washable.) Maybe you have such things already, but I imagine they are an American style.[83] Anyway, we hope you enjoy them.

In the same box we put some pecans from our yard and a few little "pocket-packs" of Kleenex, since they are new in this small size and since you liked Kleenex when you were here. Have you ever thought again of manufacturing something similar in France? Also in the box are two potato and carrot peelers which Alden Mauffray[84] asked me to include for you. You must have talked about them when he was in Paris. They are wonderful kitchen help!

I'm enclosing a snapshot and two clippings you'll be interested in. Thank you for your snapshots. Do please send the others.

Arlette, the last remnant of the old bridge was removed this week. The bay and sand beach look much prettier now.

Everyone joins me in love to you all, and once again: Merry Christmas!

Emily

P.S. You asked about gifts for us. Anything you send, we will love!

* * * * *

[From Venie de Montluzin)]

Feb. 26, 1954

My dear Arlette,

It was nice enough just hearing from you at Christmas time let alone receiving that delicious box of confections which we all enjoyed so very much. They had a unique flavor which was very pleasing to the palate, the flavor being something like burnt almond. A very long time ago we used to get Hylers candy

---

[83] The gifts were soft, warm bedroom slippers with knee-length wool socks attached.

[84] A Bay St. Louis friend who owned a hardware store and who had recently visited the Delattres in Paris

from N.Y. It was something like that except Hylers was chocolate with that delicious filling inside.

Thank you Arlette darling not only for the gift but for the sweet card too.

René Sr. has asked me to thank you for the beautiful book of the French Riviera. He has enjoyed so much reading it and looking at the wonderful pictures.

I was happy to find it was also written in English to familiarize me with those lovely places.

Isn't this a beautiful world and to think in our span of life we are not able to see but little of it.

Some people who could travel and do not—I can not understand. My hope and prayer is that little Lorraine will be able to take a European trip with her father & mother some day.

She is so smart, Arlette. I wish you could know her as of today. Emily will have lots to tell you about her drawings and painting. We really think she has talent.

She will spend the night with me tonight as René & Emily are going to the Carnival ball (here). She and I are going as spectators.

René Sr. is not so well today. However he is much better. Hope to have him up & out tomorrow. We think he is wonderful for his age (88). He is still "cock of the walk" if you know what I mean, but we love him very much.

The coast is beautiful now with the four lane highway and our wonderful new bridge. The new road extends from Henderson Point to Biloxi with a sand beach as long. The flowers are blooming everywhere this time of year.

You have no idea how often we think of you Arlette, your mother and Jojo and wish so much to have you with us.

Many thanks again to you with gratitude and affection from all of us to all of you,

Affectionately,
Venie de M.

* * * * *

Bay St. Louis
April 11, 1954

My dear Arlette,

As usual, we were all delighted to receive your letter and have talked about it ever since it came. But we are <u>furious</u> with you because your postscript was so tantalizing: "Maybe next time I'll tell you about my sweetheart. This time it is serious, I think." !!!!! How could you be so cruel, telling us only that much and no more? You must write immediately again and tell us all about him, or we won't forgive you! Tell us his occupation, his name, how he looks, how you met him, what he likes, how old he is—in fact, <u>everything</u>! You are our little sister, and we could not possibly be <u>more</u> interested! [. . .]

[Emily discusses Lorraine's continued interest in drawing and painting and encloses a newspaper clipping showing her beside one of her paintings on exhibit at a local art show.] Right now she is across the table from me, drawing a sketch of the Eiffel Tower! I can see the curved base and the two platforms very clearly. She talks about Paris and London and Venice—Holland and Switzerland and Spain—as if she were a seasoned European traveler! (She has a very good book telling of the travels of a child through these countries, and she likes for me to read it to her over and over again.) [. . .]

Nowadays our thoughts are all on Indochina—especially, of course, on Dien-bien-phu. Our radios, our magazines, our newspapers are full of the heroic defense and the stubborn genius of de Castries. If the fort can be held the rest of this week, the crisis will probably be over, don't you think?[85] But the whole

---

[85] Dien Bien Phu, the French army's most heavily fortified forward base in Indochina, was constructed on low ground, surrounded by jungle and mountains perfect for hiding General Giap's thousands of guerrilla attackers, who closed in around Dien Bien Phu on February 5, 1954. Because of its remote, inaccessible location, the fortress could only be reinforced by an airlift of men and supplies. The main Vietminh attack began on March 15, 1954; and fighting continued for seven weeks, with the French holding out through the month of April in hopes of overwhelming American air strikes, air strikes that never came. Colonel Christian de Castries was finally compelled to surrender on May 7, 1954, and his surviving soldiers were marched off to Vietminh prison camps, where over 7,000 of the 12,000 prisoners of war would die. The disaster at Dien Bien Phu would cost France not only seventeen battalions but, effectively, its hopes to hold on to its colonial empire in Indochina.

Indochina situation seems so hopeless. What do you think the solution can be? The outlook seems very gloomy, from any viewpoint.

I've begun reading *Gigi* and find it delightful. I saw the book and remembered your saying Colette is your favorite author; so I thought I'd find out why! I wish the book were not an English translation, but even so it is enchanting. *Julie de Carneilhan* is also included in the same volume. We were glad you told us what movies you've seen recently. I suppose you know that *From Here To Eternity* won most of the Hollywood Oscars this year. It's a very unpleasant picture and not at all typical of Army life, but the acting and direction are excellent. I still think *Moulin Rouge* is the best picture we've seen in years—except, perhaps, *Quo Vadis*, which is superb, too. We were so interested in what you told us about your work on the Lautrec reproductions, and we'd be more than delighted to receive a set of them.

I wish you could see our flowers. We love to work outside in our yard, and it's beginning to look very pretty now. When the drugstore is closed on Wednesday afternoons, all three of us usually spend those hours digging, planting, etc.—or, in René's case, cutting grass.

Dot and Dan Russell have just finished building a pretty brick house directly across the street from ours and will move into it next week. That will be especially good for Lorraine, because she will now have a playmate almost exactly her own age. You remember Dale as a baby—she's a lovely little girl of almost six now.

Speaking of moving, Mother and Harry have just moved, too—from Dallas, Texas, to St. Louis, Missouri. Harry's whole office was transferred to St. Louis. I wish it had been to New Orleans!

I know your mother must be so sad whenever she thinks of Maurice and of her little Dorothée, whom she hardly had a chance to know at all [. . .].

All of us are quite well. I'm studying Spanish every night, since there are many people living here now who have fled from Communism in Guatemala—

and consequently we now have lots of Spanish-speaking friends.[86] It's a very good opportunity for me to practice speaking with them. René has built up an ever-increasing volume of business at the drugstore and works very hard, but is always full of fun and so sweet and considerate. "Papa" and "Mamère," as Lorraine calls them, have slowed down considerably, but are feeling well enough, I believe. Papa broke a finger 3 weeks ago. A window fell on it. It's much better now.[87]

Please give our love to your mother and to Georges, and even if you have to catch another cold, please find time to write us very soon about your new friend! Even a short note will do!

All my love,
Emily

* * * * *

Bay St. Louis
October 17, 1954

My dear Arlette,

You don't know how much all of us enjoyed your long letter this summer and how much we've appreciated your taking the time to send us so many cards during your vacation trip. The scenes on the cards were beautiful, and I can imagine how you must have come home refreshed and happy after seeing so many wonderful sights. I was especially glad to see the view of the Castle of Chillon on Lake Leman, because I have always liked Lord Byron's *The Prisoner of Chillon*, which I'm sure you are familiar with. Had you ever traveled in Italy

---

[86] The Guatemalan refugees living on the Gulf Coast had fled their country after the president of Guatemala, Jacobo Árbenz Guzmán, had in 1952 enacted Decree 900, which confiscated land from large estates and parceled it out to peasant farmers, an action that especially affected the United Fruit Company's extensive plantations in Guatemala.

[87] As he was helping to lock the drugstore for the night, a heavy window, propped up in those pre-air-conditioning days, fell onto one of his fingers. Summoned at once, the family doctor hurried to the drugstore, set the broken bone, improvised a splint with two tongue depressors and adhesive tape, and congratulated René, Sr., on his fortitude.

before? I know it is a lovely country to see, but I have often wondered how it would affect me to go there and see such extremes of wealth and poverty as seem to exist there. All in all, Italy has surely been in our minds all summer—with your trip there and all the newspaper and magazine articles about such things as Italian styles, Italian movie stars, de Gasperi's death,[88] and the Wilma Montesi[89] scandal.[90] René is reading a very good historical novel now, called *Lord Vanity*, the setting of which is 18th century Venice—so, altogether, we are quite Italy-conscious! Be sure to tell us your impression of the country and the people.

We have been wondering if our friend, Mrs. John Bell, has called on you recently. I had wanted to write you that she might stop in Paris on her way from England to Italy this month, but I have been too involved with various affairs to sit down and write. She is in Europe now buying English woolens and Italian silks for an importing business she and her husband have begun. She remembers you very well, and perhaps you'll remember her if you see her. She and John were the founders of our Little Theater, and I'm sure they were here the day you painted that board or two! If she can spare the time to stop a little while in Paris, she wants very much to call you [. . .].

We have discussed your last letter many times. We feel so sorry that you and your mother and Georges must struggle against such financial burdens as [. . . have been] imposed upon you. It is terrible, and I know there are times when you are thoroughly discouraged. I hope your legal advisers can help you to find the best solution—if there is one that's good! It looks as if, under Mendès France, your country is beginning a new era of prosperity, which will no doubt be reflected in your business. Maybe one day all these problems will be settled and you can keep for yourselves the profits you three are working so hard to earn.

---

[88] Emily refers to Alcide de Gasperi, former Italian prime minister (1945-53) and, together with Robert Schuman in France and Konrad Adenauer in Germany, a champion of the European Union.

[89] Italian actress whose body had been found on the beach at Ostia the preceding year, leading to accusations of foul play and scandal involving political circles

[90] Emily's detailed knowledge of international affairs, so evident in this as in her other letters, reflects the extensive coverage of foreign news provided in the 1940s and 1950s by the print media (including her favorite magazines, *Time* and *Life*), radio broadcasts, and Fox Movietone newsreels. Such coverage would be matched in recent times only by the resources of the internet.

Speaking of your prime minister, his name is on almost every tongue over here! He is surely a miracle-worker. (Or incredibly lucky?) At any rate, France seems to have in him a firm leader once again, and we are very glad for the French people and of necessity filled with admiration for all Mendès has accomplished.[91] Tell us how you feel about him. I notice in this week's papers that he seems to have won over de Gaulle too.[92]

I'm enclosing some rather dim snapshots I took of Lorraine one day this summer on the beach. I wish you could see what a good little beach we now have. Perhaps these pictures will give you some idea of it—also of how Lorraine is growing. She's in the first grade and learning now to read. Her subjects include reading, writing, arithmetic, science, health, art, French, and dancing. Quite a schedule for a six-year-old, *isn't it?* She attends a private Episcopal school built since you were here. I take her there just before nine in the mornings and don't see her again until I go back to get her at three in the afternoon! You can imagine how we miss her during those hours, especially at lunch time [. . .].

I know you'll be glad to know that René has begun taking a holiday once a week. On Wednesday he leaves the drugstore at noon and doesn't return to it until the next morning! Consequently, we have one afternoon and evening to do as we please, for a change. For instance, last week we (René and I) went to New Orleans to do shopping that day, had dinner in a lovely restaurant in the French

---

[91] Pierre Mendès France, a center-left Radical, had succeeded Joseph Laniel on June 18, 1954, forming the fifteenth ministry of the Fourth Republic. Prior to launching progressive programs to stimulate French agriculture and industry, he had embarked on determined efforts to cut the Gordian knot of the problems that had bedeviled preceding ministries, first, securing an armistice in Indochina, with an independent Laos and Cambodia and a Vietnam partitioned at the 17th parallel (July 1954); second, proclaiming a liberal home-rule policy for Tunisia (August 1954); and third, allowing René Pléven's unpopular proposal for integrated Franco-German military units in the European Defense Community (EDC) to be shelved permanently by the Assembly (August 1954). Ironically the Paris Accords of October 1954 would bring about German military participation in the European Union after all and would lose Mendès France a great deal of political support. However, immediately before Emily wrote her letter, Mendès France was still regarded in France and abroad as, in her own words, a miracle worker, and "*Mendésisme*" was enjoying its high-tide of popularity.

[92] Charles de Gaulle had agreed to meet with Mendès France, and the conversation had taken place on October 13, four days before Emily wrote her letter. However, de Gaulle continued to hold himself aloof from endorsing Mendès France's policies, remaining instead in political opposition.

Quarter, and saw the new movie *Rear Window*, which stars James Stewart and Grace Kelly. This week we took the whole family in to New Orleans again to see Mrs. Sporl [. . .]. We spoke of you and wished for you. René says he remembers all the martinis we had that day before our dinner at Antoine's! Ada served us a delicious supper. Junior was in Chicago, so we didn't see him.

Next month Sonja Henie will be in N.O. with an ice show, which we hope to take Lorraine to see—on a Wednesday! So you can see our little holidays will mean much pleasure to us as time goes on.

You'll be interested to know that Flora and Alden Mauffray have bought a two-story pink stucco house on the beach about a block or two past the Reed Hotel. I understand the price of $31,000 included all the furnishings. I'm glad for them that they have a pretty home at last [. . .].

All of us are well and busy, We think of you <u>so</u> often [. . .]. [Emily closes with customary affectionate messages to all the family.]

As always,
Emily

Arlette dearest,

I thought perhaps this page should be separate.

We have thought so much about your present love-affair, if one can call it that correctly. You asked what we would feel about the question of his being a divorcé. The religious objection felt by Catholics would not trouble <u>us</u>, of course—nor you, either. But do you know the <u>reason</u> for his divorce? Is it something that would not affect <u>your</u> marriage, do you think? Of course, you must have thought of this from every viewpoint, and if you love him and have decided to marry him, we trust your judgment and wish you both every happiness. Please let us know more as to what the current situation is. It has been about 2 or 3 months since you wrote, and much can happen in such a long time! So write <u>soon</u>! We are dying to hear more!

I embrace you,
Emily

[Emily encloses a twice-folded photograph of a model wearing a fashionable dress, evidently torn from a magazine and marked with several notations and her name. She had written at the bottom "This picture has been to China and back!" On a slip of note paper she explains: "This is a picture of one of my new summer dresses, made for me in Hong-Kong! Mary Cannon Bell and John Bell visited Hong-Kong two years ago, were impressed with the beautiful sewing done by Chinese tailors, and started a small importing business that has grown into a large one. They set up a tailor in business there with a big shop and many workers, hired an agent in Hong-Kong, and in nine states in <u>this</u> country they have almost 80 representatives calling on people to show samples of materials and take orders for dresses and suits! You simply select a picture from any magazine, they take your measurements, and in a month you receive your dress by air express! The materials are beautiful Italian silks, Irish linens, and English woolens and cashmeres. My dress is sky-blue linen trimmed in white, and it fits beautifully. It would have cost much more in a store in the U.S."]

* * * * *

Bay St. Louis
June 3, 1955

Our dear Arlette,

I feel so ashamed that I have allowed so may months to pass by without writing to you—but our life is so full and busy that the days rush on before we realize it, and weeks slip into months and are gone. If I could only be satisfied with writing a two- or three-page letter to you, I'm sure I would write more often––but I like to write <u>volumes</u>, the way <u>you</u> do, and I always wait for a time when I'll have hours of free time. (Apparently such a time exists only in my dreams!) Today I'm determined to mail you a letter, though; and since Lorraine is sleeping late, I'm beginning this immediately after breakfast, with dishes still unwashed and beds still unmade.

We were delighted to receive your long letter and to hear all about Jacques and your wedding plans. I wish we knew Jacques, and of course I feel sure that some day we <u>shall</u>. Be sure to send us as many pictures as you can of your wedding. We think we'll write an account of it for one of our local papers. (We have another newspaper here now which we like much better than the *Echo*.) I know all your Bay St. Louis friends will be most interested in hearing of your wedding. By the way, what is Jacques' last name? As I addressed this envelope a moment ago, I thought "This will probably be the last time I'll write "Mlle Arlette Delattre"! From now on it will be "Mme Jacques ———" and I realized you've never told us his other name!

Be sure to let us know the exact date of the wedding (Is July 22 definitely set?) so we can be thinking of you both especially that day. You must know that we are all very happy for you and that we wish you every joy in your marriage. From all you have written about Jacques, he must be an ideal fiancé—for example, you said *"I have the most adorable of fiancés"*—*"Jacques is very nice and has been a great consolation to me."*—*"If I had not had Jacques, I was losing interest completely in everything."*—*"Mama is happy to see that my fiancé is an excellent man"*—etc., etc., etc.!! So we feel sure that you are as much to be congratulated as he is!

Your wedding dress sounds beautiful. I know you will be the loveliest of brides. And your plans of a honeymoon in Rome and Capri sound like a wonderful dream. By the way, we sent you a small package by airmail three days ago—just a little gift to add to your trousseau—I hope it will have reached you safely by the time this letter does. I wish we knew something you'd particularly like as a wedding gift. We are hoping that you and Jacques have been successful in your efforts to rent the wing of the English manor house you mentioned. It would be so much pleasanter to live there, of course, than in a tiny apartment in Paris. And how happy your mother and Georges would be to have you both near them! Let us know how the matter has been settled.

I could keep writing pages and more pages about such an interesting topic as your wedding, but my letter would be entirely too long. I wish you were here tonight! We would sit up and talk from now until morning! (It's now eight o'clock. I'm writing again after a meal, but this time the supper dishes are all done!)

We were all tremendously interested in your account of your business troubles and how they have been solved. We feel that you and your mother and

Georges have been most admirable in your efforts to save your firm, and that you made the wisest decision possible in selling under such favorable conditions. I am sure Jacques would not have advised you to do anything which would not be to your advantage. The terms sound very generous to us, and I know that you are all more carefree now that the heaviest responsibilities are no longer on your shoulders [. . .].

    I wish you could see our lovely beach now, Arlette [. . .]. Dot Russell and I were remembering how you used to sun-bathe on the tiny strip of sand in front of the hotel. "*La Péninsule d'Arlette*," as René always calls it. The beach was <u>very</u> nice last summer, as I wrote you before, but during the last few months the city has spent many thousands of dollars making it <u>much</u> wider and longer, scraping it to make it smooth and sandy, placing dozens of swings and other playground equipment for children there, and setting out benches for adults. Now they are spending $40,000 more on tons and tons of clay to widen the road along the top (for parking cars) and terrace the slope down to the beach, so that one can easily go down to the sand at any point along the street. It will make Bay St. Louis much more attractive to tourists as well as more pleasant for its townspeople. Lorraine loves the beach and is getting quite brown already. School has been out for two weeks now, and she is delighted to be free! I wish you could see how very well she reads—rapidly, surely, and with expression and understanding. She had a remarkably good teacher this year and we feel that she made excellent progress. She wrote you a note just before school was out, which I must enclose in this letter. It must be hard for you to realize how your "*poupée rose*" has grown! I have no new pictures to send, but I'll take some for you soon.

    We still see a movie at least once a week and have found some very good ones this year. We enjoyed *Désirée* especially (Did you read the book?) and the English production of *Julius Caesar* with James Mason as Brutus and Marlon Brando as Mark Antony. Jules Verne's *Twenty Thousand Leagues under the Sea* was excellent, too. (By the way, Mr. de Montluzin says that Jules Verne was a personal friend of <u>his</u> father!)[93]

You may have seen in the *Echo* (I had the spelling of your name corrected, incidentally!) that Mr. de Montluzin had double pneumonia last month. He has completely recovered, however, thanks to penicillin. He still enjoys coming to the drugstore to see his friends, and he gets much pleasure from Lorraine and from his television set. His health is really remarkable. He will be 90 years old in December, you know!

As much as I have heard of *East of Eden*, I have not read it. I shall, though, on your recommendation. In order not to forget what French I know, I read short stories occasionally after I go to bed—usually classic authors from college schoolbooks! I read one of de Maupassant's the other night—*Le Père Milon*—which impressed me so much with the deep hatred of Germans that must be in so many French hearts that I had to read it aloud to René. We both wonder how the "Be Friends With Germany" program will get along. Of course it would be wonderful if it really works out—and perhaps it will, since it is obviously so practical. What do <u>you</u> think? We were heartsick when Mendès France was ousted, and we spent days almost cursing the French political system that permits changes of government every month or so,[94] but perhaps it will all work out all right. Mendès had caught our imagination and commanded our respect, though, and we did hate to see him go. I hope he gets back in again!

I was talking to Effie McCulloch and Margaret Shadoin about you and Jacques today, and they wish you much happiness. Effie has a perfectly beautiful new home—every thing electrical that you can imagine!

---

[93] When Ludovic de Montluzin was a young man in Paris, prior to his emigration to America, he worked for a time as an historical researcher for Alexandre Dumas, *père*, and was also a friend of Victor Hugo, whose influence led him to take part in Hugo's unsuccessful barricade-fighting against Louis Napoleon's *coup* of 1851.

[94] Mendès France, assailed from all sides after the outbreak of the Algerian revolt in November 1954, had been ousted in a no-confidence vote on February 5, 1955. After several weeks of political interregnum, he would be succeeded on February 23 by Edgar Faure, head of the sixteenth of the twenty-one ministries of the Fourth Republic.

Remember how you taught me the French word for "hydrangeas"—"hortensias," wasn't it? We have some lovely ones in bloom now, and I often think of you when I see them—and of the beautiful ones in your father's painting. I'm so glad Mme Delattre has time now to enjoy her flowers. René and I love our big yard, and he keeps it looking beautiful. He likes to work outdoors as a change from his drugstore work. He has built up a very large business and increased his stock a great deal since you were here. We have a clerk now who is a big help to us.

I <u>must</u> <u>not</u> go on to another page! Please give your mother a kiss for me and tell her we are so happy she is soon to have another son and Georges an older brother again. I know how busy you will be this month, but do write us a <u>one-page</u> letter, at least, telling us for sure the wedding date and place.

All our love,
Emily

[From Lorraine, printed on a page of unlined tablet paper]
[June 3, 1955]

Dear Arlette,

Can you believe that I am already seven years old? I am finishing my first year in school this month, and I like reading, art, French, and music best of all my studies. Some day I am going to visit you and Jacques!

Love,
Lorraine

*   *   *   *   *

[From Emily to Camille Delattre]
Bay St. Louis
July 18, 1955

Dear Mme Delattre,

I am thinking of you today while writing to Arlette, because I know the sadness as well as the joy in your heart as the day of her marriage approaches.

We are happy that you are not alone; like my own mother on the day of <u>my</u> marriage, you will not have your adored husband at your side, but your dear son will be your comfort and will share your happiness. And then you will have another son, and Jojo an older brother again! Surely it will be a <u>good</u> <u>day</u> for you!

I send you the best regards of all the family, who so regret not being able to be present at the wedding.

Emily

*   *   *   *   *

Bay St. Louis
July 18, 1955

Arlette dear,

In four more days you will be <u>Madame Baron</u>—and I wanted to write you once more before your wedding day. I imagine that this letter will reach you on the day before your marriage, and I shall write only a little so that you'll have time to read it!

In fact, this letter is as much for Jacques as it is for you—to tell him how sincerely we welcome our "new cousin" into our family, and how much we hope that we shall meet him <u>soon</u>, either in Bay St. Louis or in Paris. We would all give anything to be present at the wedding, and you may be sure that we shall be there in our hearts and thoughts. I am sure the ceremony will have quiet simplicity and dignity, which is in my opinion more impressive and sweeter to remember than a big wedding with many bridesmaids and much excitement. Your dress is <u>beautiful</u>—<u>you</u> are beautiful—and when you have that special radiance reserved for a girl on her wedding-day, I am sure you will look lovelier than you ever have before in all your life! Be sure to send us a good picture for our newspapers.

When you have time later to write us, please tell us what you would advise us to do about a wedding gift for you and Jacques. We were horrified to think of the $13.00 duty you had to pay on a nightgown that cost only that much at the store! We had thought of sending you some gift in silver—but now we would not dare to. Would it be best to send you some money and let you buy something there in France? We want you to have something in your home that will always remind you of the love of your faraway cousins.

We have read and reread your last letters, and I'll really answer them some other time. This one is strictly about wedding affairs!

We hope every detail about your honeymoon trip to Italy will be perfect, and that you'll find a little house at once when you return to Paris. All of us send much, much love to you both and wish you a future full to the brim with happiness.

I embrace you, my little sister,
Emily

V

The End of the Story

Written by Emily de Montluzin, with Emily Lorraine de Montluzin

It would be another eleven years of letters crisscrossing the Atlantic before René, Lorraine, and I would see Arlette again. During those years, inevitably, the families lost three of their older generation.

On May 9, 1956, I wrote:

Dearest Arlette,

This is just a note to tell you that our family has had a terrible tragedy this week and I wanted to let you know as soon as possible. Mrs. de Montluzin, our very dear "Mamère," died Monday morning, May 7th, from a heart attack, a thrombosis. She had been feeling heaviness and pain around her heart for two days, and on Sunday night our local doctor advised taking her to a New Orleans hospital for examination by a heart specialist. She arrived in New Orleans about midnight,[1] and at 8:45 the next morning while the nurses were giving her her morning care and telling her how much better she was looking, she passed away almost from one instant to the next—they said it was like blowing out a candle. She was, as you know, so sweet and kind—so truly good to everyone—that the whole town is grief-stricken over her death. Papa is very brave and is remarkably composed most of the time. René, Jr., adored his mother, and I feel as much grief for him and for myself as I do for Papa—we all miss her terribly—even little Lorraine, who of course cannot yet realize her loss. Papa is now with us, though he can go home often, and we won't shut that house up at all.

We have been a little uneasy about you and your family since we have not heard from you since Christmas. Hope you've just been busy. Our love to all of you.

Emily

When René, Sr., came across the street to live with René, eight-year-old Lorraine, and me, he did so with admirable fortitude and brought with him only his canary and his cat. The guest room was now his room, filled with familiar furniture from the old home, and from time to time he walked across the street again to sit on his porch and look out at the bay. Lorraine was a great joy to him, as were visits of relatives and friends. He often rode to the drugstore and kept in touch with customers and new aspects of the business. He felt well, and the next two years of his life were pleasant ones. But on November 14, 1958, I wrote:

> [O]n Sunday morning, October 19th, René and I awakened hearing a strange, croaking sound and realized after a few moments that it came from Papa's room. He had had a stroke of paralysis and had lost his

---

[1] By ambulance, accompanied by René and the family doctor

speech and all movement in his left side, and he was trying to call us. By the time the doctor came, in about ten minutes, he was gasping for breath and filling up with a heavy fluid in his throat and bronchial tubes. Of course the doctor said he must be taken at once to the hospital, but when the ambulance came, he pleaded so pathetically with his eyes and pushed the man away with his right hand— obviously begging to stay at home—that René and the doctor agreed it would be best to let him stay if the necessary equipment could be obtained from the hospital. So we have a hospital bed for him, a suction apparatus to draw out the fluid from his throat, and three nurses on 8-hour shifts. For the first week we were all <u>sure</u> he was dying—in fact, six times we all gathered at his bed thinking the end had come—but each time he would drive death away and keep on breathing. Gradually his agonized breaths grew easier, and the deep coma he was in for many days lightened, and he began to have periods of consciousness. At last he was able to say a word or so again, and we have rejoiced over each word as if he were a baby learning to speak his first ones. For 18 days his only nourishment was dextrose and water, given intravenously because, since his throat muscles were paralyzed, he could not swallow at all and the doctor could not get a nasal feeding tube down into his stomach. But a week ago today the tube finally was inserted, and since then he has had beef bouillon, milk, orange juice, and a meat-base baby food through the tube. He is conscious now all the time and can speak a few words occasionally in a hoarse, guttural way—but he is still in a terrible condition and realizes it. He cannot even shift his position in bed or pull the cover up or push it down. He still cannot swallow, really, though he sometimes manages to get a few drops of water or Coca Cola down when it is placed on his tongue with a medicine dropper. He cannot hold a pencil to write what he wants, and sometimes he tries for hours to say something, and just can't do it. We still have the nurses 24 hours a day, and Mrs. de Montluzin's two sisters (Mrs. Crebbin and

Miss Word), who are graduate nurses, you know, have come over many times to help us. You will be interested to know that the only way Papa can communicate with us really is through Lorraine. He can use his right hand a little, and several years ago, just for fun, he had taught her the deaf-mute alphabet, or sign language, using the fingers of the right hand for each letter. Now, when he is not too weak, he sometimes spells out words to her, and she acts as our interpreter.

You can imagine how hard these past weeks have been for us all. We had to make up our minds to <u>lose</u> him, and, as he improved a little, we have had to make up our minds to face a pathetic <u>future</u> for him. If he continues to improve, it will be wonderful, but if he can't move or talk or swallow, life will be torment for him. Time will tell the answer.

I added, "We have followed avidly every word of news about France and de Gaulle for many months and are so glad he is at the head of the government.[2] Tell us how the situation looks from <u>inside</u> France. French news is the only kind that interests Papa at all."

In a letter of February 2, 1959, I reported on Papa's improving condition, though he was still confined to his bed and still had constant nursing care. I then continued:

> I know you'll all be <u>astonished</u> to hear that we have received a few words <u>personally</u> from <u>General de Gaulle</u>! I can hardly believe it myself—but this is how it happened: Ever since Papa became ill, he has been interested in <u>nothing</u> <u>at</u> <u>all</u> except news of France and especially of de Gaulle. When I read to him any magazine story about

---

[2] Charles de Gaulle had become premier of France on June 1, 1958, and had formed the last of the 21 ministries of the Fourth Republic. Using the decree powers the exhausted and desperate Chamber of Deputies had given him, he presided over the rewriting of the constitution and the resultant creation of the Fifth Republic, with its appreciably strengthened executive. He would be inaugurated its first president in January 1959.

de Gaulle, he laughs and cries with emotion, and he feels that de Gaulle is the savior of France. So, on the day before de Gaulle was elected president, I wrote to him on a sudden impulse (and quickly, before I lost my courage!). I told him I wanted to bring him greetings from one of his oldest and most fervent admirers in the U.S.—and I told him a little about Papa's French background, his age, his illness, and how he feels about de Gaulle. I ended by saying that Mr. de Montluzin wished to send him greetings at Christmas and his hopes that de Gaulle would have many years of successful guidance of *la belle France*. Then, amazed at my own temerity, I mailed the letter to Colombey-les-Deux Églises[3] and hoped that, at the most, a secretary of de Gaulle might read it and send a note which I could show Papa and say, "Look! This came from de Gaulle's own office!"

But I never dreamed Gen. de Gaulle would take the time to reply himself—and he did! Isn't that wonderful, as busy as he is, and with so many problems on his mind! Two weeks ago his reply came—a small airmail letter, addressed in a feminine handwriting in blue ink, and stamped *"Président de la République."* Inside was a personal calling card, engraved very simply *"Général de Gaulle,"* and under his name was written in black ink and a bold, masculine handwriting *"Avec ses remerciements et ses meilleurs voeux."*[4]

You can imagine Papa's pleasure and pride. We are so grateful that such a great man would be kind enough to acknowledge such a note himself.

---

[3] The village in eastern France where de Gaulle's private home was located
[4] *"With his thanks and his best wishes."*

[Emily enclosed for Arlette the original handwritten draft of the letter which she had copied and sent to Charles de Gaulle.[5] She had deliberately written it in English, reasoning that that would attract more attention in de Gaulle's office than a letter written in French. (Edit.)]

It was on February 20 that René wrote to the family in France to tell them of his father's death:

> Dear Arlette and Jacques, Mme Delattre, Georges, and Cousin René,
> Just a short note today to let you know that my darling Papa passed away quietly Wednesday afternoon about five-forty-five. Although he had improved a great deal since the onset of his illness, in the last two weeks he had had two additional strokes which weakened him greatly. Then Wednesday afternoon about three o'clock he had a final stroke. He had suffered so much, yet he was a good patient and tried so hard to cooperate with our efforts to help him.
>
> You know that when he was born in 1865 his father wrapped the baby in a French flag; so it was most appropriate that one of our

---

[5] The following is the text of Emily's letter:

My dear General de Gaulle,
 On the eve of your election as president, I would like to bring you greetings from my husband's father, who is doubtless one of your oldest and most fervent admirers in the United States. He is René de Montluzin, Sr., ninety-three years old, and the grandson of the Lt. Louis de Montluzin who carried Napoleon's ill-fated message to General Grouchy. Ever since he suffered a severe stroke of paralysis two months ago, he has been interested in nothing except news of France; and yesterday as I read to him the article about you in *Newsweek Magazine,* he alternately laughed and cried with emotion.
 When he was born, just after his family came to Louisiana from France, his father wrapped him in a French flag—and his love for France and belief in her glory are the rocks to which he clings now in his illness.
 To him you represent all that is good and great in his country, and he wishes you a happy Christmas and years of successful guidance of *la belle France.*
  Very sincerely yours,
  Emily de Montluzin
  (Mrs. René de Montluzin, Jr.)

friends here who is Belgian sent to his funeral a small heart-shaped arrangement of blue, white, and red flowers with tricolor ribbons. We put this in his hands when he was placed in the family tomb today.

I am enclosing a clipping from the *Echo* for you to read. Emily will write you later.

My love to you all,
René

As I wrote to Arlette on April 16, 1959:

He seemed indestructible, like a landmark on the Gulf Coast, and it is incredible that he is gone. During his last years he used to say, "Now that I'm old, I don't have any friends left—No one cares a damn about me!" But he would have been so pleased to see how many people were affected by his death, how many friends sent flowers, wrote letters, and sent donations to Lorraine's school or to various charities in his memory. In fact, I have written more than 250 notes acknowledging these expressions of sympathy. And of course many, many friends came to visit us in person and talk about the old days when he was young and the things they could remember about him. I wish you could have attended his Masonic funeral; my father had one too, and the service is impressive and beautiful. Since Papa felt as he did about church-going, we did not have a religious service at our church, as that would have been a farce; but our minister (you remember him, Arlette, don't you?) was his personal friend and a Mason also; so he and other Masons, some of whom had known Papa for more than half a century, took charge of his burial. It had rained all night the night before, but that morning the sun came out brightly and the little cemetery was full of his friends.

Five years later it was the turn of René Delattre, the last of the older generation, to leave the family. I wrote to Arlette in November, 1964, that in February René and I had received a letter from him, reminiscing about the days when he was a young man and his *"Oncle Ludovic et Tante Reine"* had emigrated to America. He described his small apartment, where he lived alone and enjoyed his television, even such American programs as *Father Knows Best (Papa Avait Raison)* and the comedies of Laurel and Hardy. As for himself, he wrote, *"I go clip-clop with my faithful cane. I move a little faster than a snail, for my legs have lost their speed. I don't think I'll take part now in the Olympic games in Tokyo."* Again reliving the past, he said, *"They have revived at the Comédie Française* Cyrano de Bergerac. *We saw* Cyrano *in 1900 with Corinne, my brother Georges, and me. . . . All that's far away. . . . It's passed like water under a bridge. . . ."* And he closed his letter with these words: *"Well, my friends, we are going to leave you. I wish you long, happy years, as well as little Lorraine, who has a lot of future before her. . . . As for me, I'm near the end. Many good kisses, René, . . . the last of the Mohicans of the old family."*

We had continued unceasingly with plans for our long-hoped-for trip to Europe, plans put on indefinite hold when *my* René was stricken by a rare, catastrophic, and never-diagnosed illness attended by partial paralysis. Experimental treatment prescribed by specialists at Ochsner Hospital in New Orleans saved his life and enabled him to return to work, but it would be years before he fully recovered. As I wrote to Arlette:

> It is a wonderful thing to live in a small town, where almost everyone is a friend who is deeply concerned over such an illness. We are, as you know, Episcopalians—but when René was so sick, prayers were made for him in the hearts of Catholics, Baptists, Methodists, and Jews, Presbyterians and Lutherans, white people and black people— and many a Mass was said for him in Catholic churches here and in

New Orleans, special prayers in our own church, and even in a Jewish synagogue in New Orleans. And once [. . . early one Sunday morning], after he came back from Ochsner's, he had to go back to the hospital here because his hemoglobin [. . .] count had fallen dangerously low. He was given six pints of blood by transfusion, and when his blood type was determined, the hospital called for donors, and within 20 minutes three people were there to offer him their blood [. . .].[6] The next day others came, and though he only used six pints, almost 30 people either gave him blood or gave to the "blood bank" in his name. He has received countless letters, flowers, telephone calls, and jars of homemade preserves, etc., from well-wishers, and we have been made to realize as never before how many friends we have among both races here and all creeds and walks of life.[7]

I added with regret, "Of course, our plans to visit you in Europe have necessarily been postponed [. . .]. René says that he wants to wait until his feet are really strong enough again for him to walk gaily down the Champs-Élysées with Jacques on one arm and his beautiful French *cousine* on the other!"

By 1966 that day finally came, and in celebration of René's recovery and Lorraine's graduation from high school, we resolved at last to travel! René was able to employ a recently retired pharmacist to keep the drugstore open while he was away, and in June the three of us in our turn sailed across the Atlantic. We would see as much of Europe as we could in two months, but first, of course, would come our reunion with Arlette and our face-to-face meeting at last with the French cousins whom we knew so well through our correspondence—Georges,

---

[6] The emergency request was made from pulpits during services in various local churches that Sunday morning, and the three volunteers with René's extremely rare blood type immediately left their pews to go to the hospital and donate blood.

[7] Excerpt from Emily's letter of November 6, 1960

his wife Jeannine, their little son Frédéric, Mme Delattre, and Arlette's husband Jacques.

It was Georges we saw first as our boat train to Paris slowed down at twilight in the Gare St. Lazare—a tall, smiling young man running along beside the windows, peering in to locate us. As I wrote three years later, remembering our travels, "I began to cry when I saw you, Arlette, and you said, 'Don't cry, Emily!'" How wonderful it was to meet Georges, Jeannine, and Jacques at long last! And then we were crammed into the car, all seven of us, plus all of our suitcases, and in moments we were driving home through streets lined by floodlit sights we had pored over in books for years. I told Arlette:

> [T]he most wonderful thing of all was that we first saw Paris just at that time of night, when people were still on the streets and all the marvelous monuments and famous places like the Opéra were illuminated and brilliant. It was like a dream, driving past one after another, so quickly, with you two and Georges and Jeannine laughing and pointing to the Arc de Triomphe, the Champs-Élysées, and all the other places we had dreamed of all our lives! And then the climax came when we reached the lovely little home at 8 Avenue des Mérisiers, with its walled garden, and met Mme Delattre, who had stayed with *le petit* Frédéric and had prepared for us a banquet we shall never forget![8]

Early the next morning we began a car trip with Arlette and Jacques that took us through Alsace-Lorraine, the Swiss Alps, and the Lake Geneva countryside. On our return Arlette, who was having heart palpitations from a thyroid imbalance she had studiously avoided mentioning to us, announced that she had appointed Dorothée, now nearly Lorraine's age, as our companion and guide in Paris. Dorothée's parents, Maurice and Huguette, had only recently come back to France to live, and she had spent most of her life in Brazil, where

---

[8] Excerpt from Emily's letter to Arlette, June 17, 1969

they had moved after their early years in Argentina. Consequently she, like us, was seeing France for the first time and sharing in our excitement.

Trips by train or bus to the Loire Valley, southern France, Rome, Venice, and Florence followed; and we had the excitement of celebrating Bastille Day in Paris with Arlette and Jacques, watching from reserved seats on the Champs-Élysées (a bit of miracle-working Arlette had contrived) as Charles de Gaulle himself rode past, standing at ramrod attention in his military car. How awestruck Papa would have been! Our trip ended with two weeks of intensive sightseeing on our own in southern England, a special delight to Lorraine, who was already resolved to concentrate in college on English history and literature.

Our two months abroad, so long anticipated and so often postponed, had far exceeded the hopes we had expressed over and over in our letters to Arlette. We had had the opportunity to see at last the wonderful places we had read about all our lives and the leisure to see them well. We had had the delight of being with Arlette again and of forging closer ties with the rest of our transatlantic family. I had had the pleasure of immersing myself in the language, history, and culture of France and Italy, invaluable preparation for my as-yet-unforeseen return to teaching French and Latin in the near future. René, who would write upon our return, "I live in America but my blood is French," had had the deep satisfaction of exploring for himself the land of his ancestors. And for Lorraine, our summer in Europe would provide an unsurpassable preparation for her years of study in college and graduate school and for her eventual career as a professor of eighteenth-century British and medieval European history.

As I later reminded Arlette, remembering our farewells when the boat train departed from Paris, "You wrote that when you left the Gare du Nord, Jacques said to you, '*Ne pleure pas, ma petite Lelette. Tu les reverras!*'"[9] We hope you are right, Jacques, because more than anything in the world we all three want to return and to see all of you again."[10]

---

[9] "Don't cry, my little Lelette. You will see them again!"
[10] Excerpt from Emily's letter to Arlette, June 7, 1969

In 1969 disaster devastated the Mississippi Gulf Coast when Hurricane Camille suddenly changed its predicted course hours before landfall and struck it with Category-5-force winds and surging tidal waters during the night of August 17. Dorothée had come to spend part of the summer with us, and that afternoon, when we left our beloved old drugstore, resting on its pilings on the water side of the beach road, she helped us take home as many treasured or important items as possible—the portraits of Mamère and Papa, René's Loyola University diploma, the daybook and ledgers, the prescription files, and several framed family photos. René locked the heavy iron safe containing narcotics; Lorraine hastily filled a cardboard box with our most precious pharmaceutical antiques from the office display—the pill-making machine, mortars and pestles, the cachet-maker, the apothecary scales for weighing ingredients for prescriptions, the handwritten, turn-of-the-century "Recipe Book" of amazing nostrums dating from the drugstore's earliest days; and we drove away with a sense of inevitability through the deserted business district, past storefronts covered with plywood. We could do no more, and all that remained was to take all possible precautions at home.

Hours later the full force of the hurricane was upon us. All of our electrical power was out, and we were relying on flashlights. The wind was shrieking so loudly that we were not even aware that five of our pecan trees were falling about us. Dorothée and I were desperately hanging on to the knobs of the living-room double doors facing the beach, triple-bolted and nailed shut with plywood yet being sucked alternately in and out. Suddenly our ears were popping, and above the roar of the storm we could hear the unmistakable freight-train sound of a tornado directly above our heads. Muddy water began pouring in under the front door and bubbling up through the floor furnaces, and I instinctively ran to pull down the attic stairs in the hall as a last resort.

And then, just as suddenly, the worst was unquestionably over. The winds began to diminish, the water that had rushed in receded, and we realized that we were going to stay alive. Still in the dark we wiped our muddy feet as well as possible and collapsed into our beds, physically and emotionally drained.

It was Dorothée who woke us the following morning. She had risen first, and, resolved on the foolhardy notion of walking downtown to survey the damage, she had picked her dangerous way through debris, fallen trees, and snapping live wires, running a nail into one foot in the process. We awoke to the sound of her sobbing at our bedside, "Oh, Emily! Oh, René! The drugstore is *gone*!" Two days later I wrote to Arlette, knowing the unbearable anxiety the family felt about all of us:

> Just a note to tell you we are all safe and our home is not damaged, but our little drugstore no longer exists. It is only a pathetic jumble of debris falling down the side of the bluff. Every building except one vacant one on the water side has disappeared. Mauffray's Hardware is only half a store. Our little church is entirely gone—just vanished. So is the Yacht Club. So are most of the beautiful homes on the beach all along the Gulf Coast. Our entire town looks worse than a battlefield, with giant trees broken & splintered, houses broken, electric wires down, and people wandering about through the unbelievable debris with expressions of horror and shock. No one dreamed that a hurricane could do what this one did. The gay and beautiful Gulf Coast is totally wrecked, and hundreds of people were drowned (including, Arlette, the elderly wife of the Episcopal minister from Pass Christian who baptized Lorraine—remember?). It's all like a nightmare! I feel so sorry for René. I have thought how strange it is that the drugstore has been killed by a hurricane with a French name— And the last person who took a picture of it was a young boy named de Montluzin—a cousin from Baton Rouge who stopped there the afternoon of the tragedy. We took the portraits of Mamère and Papa home when we left for the last time, and our pictures on that wall, a few items from the display of antiques, the business record books—and that's all. We cannot realize it is all we have left.

We had a few inches of mud & water on our floors at home when the tidal wave came, but no real damage except to all our trees.

Dorothée & Lorraine have worked <u>tremendously</u> to help sweep & mop the mud out & carry out rugs to dry. We have no electricity & almost no water but plenty of food and can go get water to drink nearby. Our car is okay. I'll write more later.

Love from four lucky people,
Emily

P. S.   Dorothée & I took pictures today, but even pictures can't show such massive destruction. I forgot to tell you the old family home is still standing but roof and interior damage from rain were considerable.

Two weeks later I continued the unfolding story when I wrote again to Arlette:

We knew how deeply worried you must have been, and how frantic Dorothée's family were, but we had no way at all to send a telegram or to telephone. The first communication with the outside world beyond Bay St. Louis was the picking up and bringing in of letters <u>by helicopter</u> the day I wrote to you and she wrote to her parents.

Today, fifteen days after the hurricane, we still have no drinking water and no telephone or telegraph service, but this morning <u>at last</u> we have <u>electricity</u> again—and what a blessing it is to have lights, hot water for bathing, refrigeration, and even TV! We had never realized what luxuries such things are. We are still driving about three miles every day or two to fill containers with water from a very deep well, which is pure and safe to drink and to use for washing dishes. Until today we have cooked on a small camp stove that uses Butane fuel, and we have gone at least once a day to the Bay High cafeteria to get a good, hot meal provided for everyone by the Red Cross and cooked by the Army. The town is absolutely buzzing with soldiers, many of them in battle array, riding on jeeps and patrolling the streets to prevent looters—and many others cutting trees and hauling away debris on gigantic trucks. Thousands of huge oaks & pines were victims of the storm, and it is so strange to see the trees that remain standing either <u>leafless</u> or with <u>brown</u>, <u>dried</u> <u>leaves</u>, exactly as if it were winter. All the Spanish moss was blown away. We lost five big pecan trees at our home, but four of them fell in a semicircle about the house, forming a protective shield which caught floating debris and flying wood and saved us from great damage [. . .]. Dorothée was a great help, assisting us in quickly picking up everything on the closet floors before it got too wet and lifting the heavy color TV up onto a big table [. . .]. But on Wednesday we had an opportunity to send her to New Orleans [. . .], and she was by that time almost in a state of shock and beginning to have fever from the tetanus & typhoid shots we had all taken—so we sent her in to stay with Olga & Dick Drown, and we knew that from there she could send a cablegram to Maurice. In the meantime we had tried to send him one through a "ham" (amateur) radio operator here, but I suppose it never reached him. By the next day there were 2 emergency telephones placed outdoors downtown, and we sent Maurice another message. We felt so sorry for them, knowing their great anxiety. By the following Tuesday we were able to drive to N.O. and go to the airport with Dorothée to say goodbye, then we spent the night with our family & had a hot bath, washed our hair, ate a delicious dinner, and even went to the movies to see *Romeo and Juliet*! Lorraine said she felt better just seeing someone else's tragedy! She has been working like a farm laborer, trying to clear our yard of debris [. . .]. One of the shops along the beach is still piled in our backyard, incidentally!

We have not been able to salvage anything from the drugstore yet—the big rooftop is too heavy to move. René is thinking now that he may build another one, but not on the beach, certainly.

In the first weeks after the hurricane bulldozers and giant cranes were used to lift and load onto trucks the largest and heaviest portions of demolished buildings, and all three of us stood miserably on the sidewalk one day at the site of our drugstore and watched as the jaws of a tall red crane clamped on piece after piece of what was left and swung it around high in the air to the bed of a waiting truck. In a letter to Arlette in November René added this postscript: "I dream about our little drugstore almost every night, and Papa and Mother are with me. When the bulldozer took away the building and I saw the sign with my grandfather's name on it picked up like a piece of paper, I just couldn't keep the tears back. I miss everything so much."

He did reopen a new de Montluzin drugstore some months later, renting half of a large building on Main Street and equipping and stocking it completely but with no gold-labeled apothecary bottles, marble-topped counters, or frosted glass. Lorraine finished her senior year at Newcomb College and began graduate study at Duke University, and I continued to teach French and Latin at our high school and be active in the Little Theater. Our only sadness was the unexpected death of my mother in 1970, leaving Harry alone in St. Louis.

In August 1976 Arlette returned to Bay St. Louis, this time accompanied by her husband. As in the days of her first visit, a round of parties ensued, beginning with a reception at our home to which we invited all her friends of 1948. We had no idea that this would be the last time we would all be together, but on the evening of New Year's Day, 1977, René, sitting in his lounge chair watching the evening news, died so gently that Lorraine and I thought he had dozed off. Lorraine noticed that he was smiling. I wrote to Arlette a week later:

Dearest Arlette and Jacques,
    It breaks my heart to write this letter.

We can be thankful, though, that he must have felt no pain and that the only suffering is ours.

He had had a happy day at home, had enjoyed a very good dinner and watched a championship football game, and just before he died, he had drunk a glass of wine with Lorraine and me as we watched the evening news. I believe death was instantaneous and that he was unaware that it happened. We called an ambulance (which arrived in three or four minutes!) and he was taken at once to the hospital, where machines succeeded in getting his heart to beat again and to keep it beating for five hours before it stopped again, this time forever. But during those five hours he was in a deep coma and knew nothing at all.

We tried, as I told you, to call you for three days, although we soon realized that you were out of the city. I wish you could know how René's death has <u>shocked</u> and <u>saddened</u> our entire community. <u>Everyone</u> loved him and respected him, and Lorraine and I have been <u>surrounded</u> by loving friends and sympathy. Our church was completely overflowing at his funeral service, and our home has been overflowing all week with beautiful flowers. Every day brings dozens of letters, all of them speaking of what a <u>gentle</u>, good man he was and of how much he will be missed. I don't believe he realized how <u>much</u> he was loved and admired by everyone who knew him. We just <u>cannot</u> <u>believe</u> what has happened.

It is terribly hard for Lorraine and me to go about this empty house. And, as I told you, we decided we must (and <u>should</u>) close the drugstore, which would never be the same again without our René. So we are losing the drugstore, too, which was so big a part of our lives, also. Everything seems so unreal [. . .].

    Write to us and think of us, as we think of you.

Love,
Emily and Lorraine

    During the years following René's death Lorraine and I made numerous trips to various parts of Europe, including regions of France we had not seen before. Whenever possible we spent a few days again with our various French cousins, in Paris or in Evian on Lake Geneva, where Arlette and Jacques had built a new home. Twice again they visited us in Bay St. Louis. After I retired in 1983 from teaching at Bay Senior High School, our trips continued, and in June 2005 Lorraine in her turn took an early retirement after thirty-one years as a professor of history at Francis Marion University in Florence, South Carolina, selling her house in Florence and adding to our home a new wing encompassing an extensive study and library for full-time research.

    By that summer, Bay St. Louis had become a thriving, prosperous community, completely recovered from Hurricane Camille thirty-six years before. Families that had lost homes, and new residents alike, had built with confidence, even in low-lying areas, trusting in the latest construction techniques, elevating their houses above the danger level by building them on massive pilings. Some had reinforced those buildings with steel girders sunk into concrete and extending to the roof line, confident that the new technology would be "hurricane-proof." Painters, sculptors, and stained-glass makers had come, establishing an artists' colony of fast-growing reputation. Antique dealers and restaurateurs had followed, and Bay St. Louis, always a place of natural beauty, had become in addition a magnet for tourists, come to shop for antiques or art, enjoy its seafood festival, visit its new casino, walk on its beaches. City officials had proudly billed it as "a place apart." It had recently celebrated the tercentenary of the day in

August 1699 when the French-Canadian explorer Bienville[11] had first sailed into its bay on the feast day of St. Louis and named it in his honor, and Bienville's statue, surrounded by memorial bricks and plaques given by local families, gazed out from atop its high bluff toward the bay he had named. Then on the morning of August 29, 2005, Hurricane Katrina with its 35-foot-high tidal surge slammed into the Mississippi Gulf Coast with the force of a battering ram.

No one who had lived through Camille in 1969 had believed that any hurricane could ever be worse. Katrina put that assumption to rest. Camille's eye had been small and compact. Katrina's eye was enormous, and Bay St. Louis and Waveland were in its northeast quadrant, the most deadly zone in a hurricane's trajectory. The offshore barrier islands had afforded some protection to the coast during Camille, but Camille had left them battered and eroded; and Katrina's tsunami-like wall of water met little resistance as it swept over them. It obliterated the historic beach-front districts of Bay St. Louis and every other Mississippi Coast town, caused catastrophic human loss, and utterly destroyed the way of life that all who lived there had loved. The Bay St. Louis that we had always known simply no longer existed.

Just as Hurricane Camille had wiped away our drugstore, so Katrina demolished the gracious family home that Ludovic and Reine de Montluzin had built atop the bluff overlooking the bay. Long since sold and transformed into the elegant Bay Town Inn, it had been reduced in minutes to a heap of splintered timbers and swept away. In the words of its last owner, who had chosen to stay the night on the premises with six friends, "that wonderful old house just disintegrated" around them. All seven were flung into the branches of an enormous oak tree, ironically one that had been saved from tree cutters by Venie

---

[11] Jean Baptiste Le Moyne, sieur de Bienville (1680-1768). After sailing into and naming the Bay of St. Louis on August 25, 1699, he served as commander of France's settlement in Biloxi and later founded Mobile (1710) and New Orleans (1718).

de Montluzin when it was a sapling. Hanging onto its limbs for hours, stung by whipping winds and driven sand, and repeatedly submerged as wave followed wave, all seven survived.[12]

The debris from the old family home together with wreckage from other beach-front properties on both sides of the bay crashed into our house several hundred feet inland. Though strongly built and carapaced in protective plywood over its windows and doors, it was no match for Katrina, which peeled off its plywood coverings, shattered its plate-glass windows, and ripped its thick cypress front door off its hinges and tore it in half. Muddy salt water surged through the house to a depth of seven feet, picking up furniture, appliances, and Lorraine's library of 1,500 books, tossing them about, and leaving what remained in sodden, broken heaps. Most of our antique furniture, brought years before from the family home when we sold it, was carried out to sea. We were not there to witness the destruction; we had evacuated, reluctantly, only hours earlier, convinced that our house, which had withstood Camille, would be safe. Had we stayed, we would have been killed, drowned in muddy water or battered to death by debris.

We returned to survey the damage three weeks later. Our sidewalk was strewn with fallen limbs and downed electrical wires. Not a tree was left standing, and all of the enormous azaleas, camellias, and hydrangeas had been killed. Our lot was piled high with mounds of timber from other destroyed buildings, and three wrecked cars sat askew in the yard. Inside, our house was a shambles: interior walls were punched out, down to the bare studs in most places; torn wallpaper dangled limply in strips; the high-water mark was painfully visible in every room; shredded curtains billowed through broken windows; chandeliers, slowly corroding from salt spray, hung in place, looking down over tangled heaps of smashed furniture, flotsam from other people's homes, and a thick mat of

---

[12] Four were swept out of the tree in the tidal surge but managed to find other refuge. The remaining three—Nikki Nicholson (the owner), Doug Niolet, and Kevan Guillory—clung to the branches throughout the entire three hours until the water began to recede and they could drop to the ground, stripped of most of their clothes, stripped of their shoes, covered with abrasions from the tree bark, smeared with dark brown mud "as if dipped in chocolate," as Guillory later said, but alive.

marsh grass; viscous, blackish mud, streaked with oil from damaged offshore oil rigs, stood ten inches deep throughout the house; cross-ties from the railroad bridge and porch banisters from the Bay Town Inn lay in the mound of debris in our dining room. Clearly, as Lorraine put it, the old family home had helped kill *our* house.

We discovered that the three walls of the house that had stood through the storm had trapped a few of our favorite antiques, and we allowed ourselves to hope that they, though badly damaged, could be restored. The deep layer of mud had cushioned most of our silver, china, and crystal as it toppled from cabinets and, forming a thick smooth layer, had concealed it from the eyes of looters. The Delattre portraits and landscapes, plucked by Lorraine from the walls and stored in a high cabinet in the last hours before we evacuated, remained stacked in place, scuffed and coated with mud but, we believed, repairable.[13] Familiar pots and pans still sat unhurt under the kitchen sink, and some of our clothes, lying in soggy heaps on closet floors, could be salvaged. All but eight of Lorraine's books, however, were destroyed and would have to be replaced, if obtainable. With the help of friends we would retrieve what we could for transport to South Carolina to await restoration and eventual installation in the new house we planned to buy in Florence. To our grief, the shell of our home in Bay St. Louis was beyond saving.

Of all the losses we had suffered, the one that devastated me the most was that of our twelve large scrapbooks, filled with family photographs and newspaper clippings I had lovingly assembled for more than sixty years. We had left them carefully stored in the highest drawers of steel file cabinets, taking prudent precautions against a possible tornado, convinced that they would be safe. All the cabinet drawers were flooded; all the albums were lost.

Georges, who had already contacted us by cell 'phone in great alarm as we evacuated, had telephoned us again as soon as the enormity of Katrina's

---

[13] Several of the Delattre works, ones that had been painted on wood because wartime deprivations had made canvas difficult to obtain, were also warped. In the end, all were successfully restored except for the portrait of René de Montluzin, Sr., which was too badly damaged to repair.

destruction made headlines around the world. "Do you need money?" he had asked immediately and simply. Arlette, who knew our town so well, was in tears, mourning the loss of the *"petit Bay St. Louis"* she had cherished in memory ever since her first visit over fifty years before. Everything she remembered was gone—the old home where she had lived for two months in 1948, our home that she and Jacques had visited in later years, the beach where she had sunbathed in her bikini, the Little Theater she had helped to paint, the houses of friends who had entertained her. Like Georges, she rushed to think of how she could help. But Arlette could not talk with us to express her grief; Arlette could no longer speak.

During 2001 she had begun to develop difficulty in swallowing and in articulating words, a mystery to various specialists in Evian who were baffled by her unusual symptoms. In 2004 she had traveled to the Salpetrière Hospital in Paris, where her illness was finally diagnosed as an atypical form of ALS, commonly known as Lou Gehrig's Disease. Rare and incurable, this devastating illness usually strikes first at the extremities, paralyzing feet and hands, but in her case she remained almost to the end able to walk and to write. After surgery to insert a feeding tube she returned to Evian, where Jacques took faithful care of her at home as her condition inexorably deteriorated and she could no longer eat or speak at all. Lovely, intelligent, cultured Arlette, fluent in four languages, could not utter a word.

The catastrophe of Hurricane Katrina and the personal losses we had suffered seemed to energize her. When she realized that all our photograph albums, full of memories, must be lost, she knew that there was one concrete thing that she could do to help. Georges had already promised to send us copies of family photos and others we had sent to him from time to time, and he suggested to Arlette that she follow his example. She had never discarded a letter, clipping, or photograph that I had sent since we began our correspondence in 1945, and in his presence at her bedside, following her operation at the Salpetrière, she wrote, still legibly, that she wished to return to me every photo, every letter from our sixty-year correspondence:

My little Jojo!
This is going to put you to work: I have hundreds of photos from New Orleans and Bay St. Louis [. . .] of family and friends. At your suggestion we'll make a complete collection if the [. . .] de Montluzins have lost their family papers and memoirs—our way of reconstituting them and of helping [. . .].

What do you think of this?

At your orders, Mr. Editor-in-Chief

She wrote to me separately about her tremendous scheme, saying that her bedroom was so filled with piles of my letters and photos that it looked as if a second Bay St. Louis were spread around her bed. "In this way," she wrote, "at least I can restore your past!"

We were heartbroken that her illness was progressing toward its final stage and overwhelmed that she was thinking so generously of us. She died in 2006, at home, with Jacques and Georges at her bedside.

Time passed, and no boxes of letters arrived, though in two telephone calls Jacques had assured us that he would send them. Then he himself died suddenly in 2009 without leaving a will, and the civil authorities informed Georges that any question of inheriting Arlette's effects would depend upon an official search by a court-appointed genealogist for other possible legal heirs since Jacques and Arlette had had no children.

Immediately Georges took up a determined dual mission: to acquire, by purchase if necessary, his father's paintings, which had filled his sister's home, and to rescue from possible destruction the letters and photographs that Arlette had resolved to give to us. He would be her deputy in carrying out her wishes. It was ultimately established that an heiress had been found, an adult granddaughter completely unknown to us, the daughter of Jacques' deceased son by his first marriage. I wrote to the genealogist and through him to the heiress, explaining the connection between our family and Arlette's, describing our long correspondence, noting Arlette's promise to us after Hurricane Katrina, and asking that when the house was emptied and its contents prepared for an estate sale, my letters to Arlette be set aside and given to Georges's safekeeping, since they would have no value for her but were priceless to us. Her reply was gracious, and Georges was notified that if he drove to Evian on a specified date, he would be permitted to go into the house for thirty minutes to collect them.

It was not until March 2010 that Georges and Jeannine traveled to Evian at the appointed time and retrieved several boxes, only a portion, it transpired, of the long-awaited correspondence. The genealogist, who had himself embraced our cause, made it his personal business to locate the rest and set them aside for Georges and Jeannine, who drove for a second time across France to retrieve them. "Our boot was half full of these boxes," Georges wrote with great excitement on June 19:

> Let us tell you that all of them contain your letters and the snapshots you are waiting for: photos of Lorraine's childhood from her first year to her adolescence and your family: you, René, Mr René sr, your mother, your brother, Venie. We were happy for you to find them this week [. . .]. Would you tell us if you are interested by your letters, they are many, many! [. . .] What an amount of memories!

Georges and Jeannine began a meticulous sorting and dating of the contents to make sure that everything was in proper order, and Georges wrote:

> Dear Emily and Lorraine,
>   At last we have achieved Arlette's wishes about the "rescue" of the family souvenirs [. . .]. Unfortunately I couldn't [immediately] fulfill her wishes. The day after her decease in Evian, Jacques told me, *"As long as I live, not a thing belonging to Lélette will leave this house."* Every effort on my part was therefore useless. . . .

In due course a Federal Express truck stopped at our door in Florence and left three tightly packed boxes. We cleared the dining-room table and opened them all. Out spilled hundreds upon hundreds of photographs and slides—photos of René and me, of Lorraine at all ages, of René, Sr., and Venie, of the old house and our house, of the drugstore, of the town, of our friends and their children, of Little Theater casts, of parties and bridge games and Carnival balls; dozens of carefully folded, yellowing newspaper clippings; scores of my letters, recounting in leisurely, minute detail—or commenting upon—every event in the lives of the family in America and the family in France and the historical milieu throughout which we had lived and corresponded.

Arlette had promised us after Hurricane Katrina, "At least I can restore your past!" She had kept her word. She had given us a treasure.

Dearest Arlette!